General
Editor:
L. L. KEANE

LONGMAN
LISTENING
SERIES

INTERMEDIATE LEVEL

Listening to Maggie

LESLEY GORE

Longman

Longman Group Limited
London

Associated companies, branches and representatives
throughout the world

First published 1979

ISBN 0 582 55350 4

Printed in Great Britain by
Spottiswood Ballantyne Ltd
Colchester and London

ACKNOWLEDGEMENTS
I am grateful to Michael Scuffil for his help on the
intonation exercises; also to Professor Geoffrey Leech
and Professor Jan Svartvik for *A Communicative
Grammar of English* (Longman, 1975), which I found
very helpful during the compilation of this Unit.
I am employed by the Bell Educational Trust at the
Bell School, Cambridge.

L.G.

We are grateful to the following for permission to
reproduce copyright photographs:

Camera Press Ltd., for page 20(right); Elliott & Fry
(Bassano & Vandyk Studios) for page 20(left);
Popperfoto/UPI for page 20(middle right);
'S.P.A.D.E.M., Paris, 1979' (Stravinsky by Pablo
Picasso) for page 20(middle left).

Illustrated by John Lobham.

CONTENTS

GUIDE

WHO IS THIS UNIT FOR?	1 Learners who have studied English for about four or five years in a secondary school or who have done the equivalent (i.e. to a level just below the level required for an examination such as the Cambridge First Certificate in English examination). 2 Learners who have studied English to a higher level than this, but who find listening comprehension a particular problem. Students in the first category will usually need some help from a teacher. Students in the second category will be able to use the Unit on their own, provided they can follow the explanations in the Guide.
WHAT DOES THE UNIT COMPRISE?	1 **The Workbook.** This is needed by every student whether he or she is working with a teacher or alone. The Workbook provides – information about each exercise – instructions on how to do the exercise – pictures, words, etc. for marking or ticking, for many of the exercises. The language in the Workbook has been kept simple, so that it is comprehensible to the average student. 2 **The Cassette.** This contains the exercises, with a brief reminder before each one on how it should be done. The total playing time is 60 minutes. 3 **The Guide.** This contains – further information about the exercises, where necessary – some suggestions for further work for students working with a teacher – a key to those exercises which do not provide feedback on the cassette – the tapescript of the exercises and the natural speech samples. The Guide is for use by teachers or by students working on their own.
AIMS OF THE UNIT	1 To expose students to a variety of voices, accents and speaking styles. 2 To reinforce some of the more important or problematical features of English which will have been studied in a general English course. 3 To show how these features have a significant effect on the meaning of an utterance. 4 To introduce features of everyday spoken English which, though not difficult in themselves, are usually neglected in general courses. 5 To teach useful comprehension techniques, such as guessing the meanings of unfamiliar words and expressions from the context.
DESCRIPTION	1 The Unit is divided into five parts (see the contents list on pages iii and iv). 2 Each part contains (a) five exercises, followed by (b) recordings of natural speech recorded by people who are not actors and who are speaking spontaneously.

3 An exercise comprises:

WHAT?	WHERE?
a) *The title of the exercise* Next to the title, the symbol ⬚ is used if the learner needs to write in or mark the Workbook while doing the exercise, and the symbol ⬚ if the learner needs to speak while doing the exercise.	Workbook
b) *New words* A list of any words outside LSR 6 which appear in the exercise or in the information in the Workbook about it. If a word has several meanings, the approximate meaning in that context is given; a more precise meaning can then be explained by the teacher or looked up in a dictionary such as the *Longman Dictionary of Contemporary English*. Other words are simply listed, for handling in the same way.	Workbook
c) *Situation* This explains — often with the help of an illustration — the context for the exercises; i.e. why the people concerned are talking as they are.	Workbook
d) *Practice point* This shows, usually by means of a table, what feature(s) of English the exercise is focussing upon. Further information may be given in the Guide.	Workbook (Guide sometimes)
e) *Your aim* This explains how the exercise should be done.	Workbook
f) *Example(s)* The Workbook shows exactly how the exercise is divided between: — words on cassette (symbolised by ⬚) — words the student should say (symbolised by ⬚) — words, pictures, etc. to be marked in the Workbook (symbolised by ⬚) On the cassette, the student hears the example sentence(s). If he needs to respond orally, there is a pause on the cassette signalled by a BLEEP (and symbolised by ● in the tapescript). IT IS VITAL THAT STUDENTS WORK THROUGH SECTIONS a) – f) CAREFULLY BEFORE BEGINNING THE EXERCISE.	Workbook Cassette
g) *The exercise* i) The student responds either orally or by marking his Workbook. For oral responses, he has a suitably long pause on the cassette in which to respond, and then	Cassette (and Workbook often)

WHAT?	WHERE?
he hears the correct response on the cassette. Where responses are to be marked in the Workbook, only a short pause is left on the cassette, and the student or teacher should stop the cassette for as long as is necessary. The answers can be checked immediately the exercise is finished, or later.	
ii) Additional explanations (where necessary), the tapescript of the exercise, and the Key to any exercise which involves marking up the Workbook, are given in the Guide.	Guide

4 The Natural Speech section at the end of each of the five parts, comprises:

WHAT?	WHERE?
a) The title of the exercise ⎫ as for the b) New words ⎬ exercises c) Situation ⎭ d) Questions	Workbook Workbook Workbook Workbook
These ask the student to note down or interpret some of what he hears. All the answers entail writing in or marking the Workbook.	
e) Additional explanations, the tapescript of the spoken language and the key to the questions are in the Guide.	Guide

USING THE
MATERIAL

1 The Exercises
   a) As explained, it is vital for students to understand all the explanations in the Workbook and the example exchanges before beginning an exercise.
   b) Since the exercises are meant to *train* rather than to test, it is expected that students will usually listen to an exercise as often as they need to.
   c) Exercises may be done one at a time or in batches.

2 The Natural Speech
   a) It is again vital that students understand the explanations in the Workbook before they begin to listen.
   b) They should listen to the recording straight through in order to get the gist of what is said and to answer any general question(s) there may be.
   c) They should then listen again, stopping the cassette as necessary, to answer the more detailed questions.
   d) It will be best if they listen to the recording again, taking it in as a whole.

L. L. Keane
General Editor

Maggie Parkin, 28. Manager and owner of a small travel agency doing rather out-of-the-way tours.

Mike Smith, 48. Managing Director of Tappa Typewriters Ltd.

Christine Daley, 38. Sales Executive in Tappa Typewriters Ltd. Travels abroad quite a lot. Very efficient.

Peter Crane, 21. Canadian. Trainee Sales Executive with Tappa Typewriters Ltd. Generally works with Christine. A friend of Joanna Short.

Graham Crane. Older brother of Peter. A friend of Maggie Parkin.

Joanna Short, 20. Student at a big technical college, doing a general studies course, including geography and economics.

PART ONE   INFORMATION

Who are they talking about?

New words
a motorbike
fantastic
great   } (informal) = wonderful
superb

SITUATION

Peter has just come back from a holiday on a beautiful
Greek island. He is talking to Joanna about it.

PRACTICE POINT

Personal meaning	*Impersonal meaning*
You've probably been very busy.	50 years ago, **you** couldn't go there by plane, of course.
I don't suppose **you** got my card, did you.	When you're there, **you** relax completely.
You = the person/people being spoken to.	**You** = people in general.

1·1

YOUR AIM

Listen to Joanna and Peter. When does the word 'You'
mean the other person? When does the word 'You' mean
people in general? After each BLEEP, tick the
appropriate box.

EXAMPLES

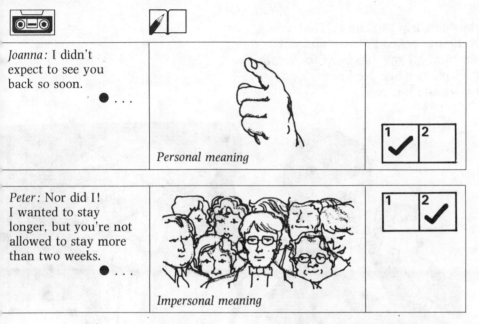

Joanna: I didn't
expect to see you
back so soon.
● ...

Personal meaning

| 1 ✓ | 2 |

Peter: Nor did I!
I wanted to stay
longer, but you're not
allowed to stay more
than two weeks.
● ...

Impersonal meaning

| 1 | 2 ✓ |

EXERCISE

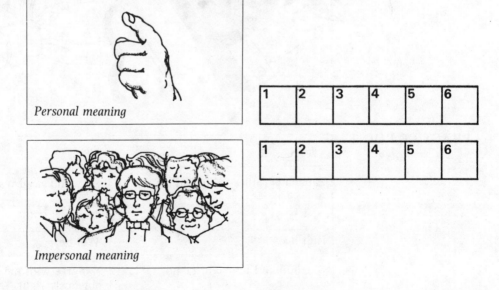

Personal meaning

| 1 | 2 | 3 | 4 | 5 | 6 |

Impersonal meaning

| 1 | 2 | 3 | 4 | 5 | 6 |

1·2

Is he asking a question, or does he just want her to agree?

New words
agricultural
mind you (informal) = however . . .

SITUATION

Mike is going on a business trip to Zanada. He has not been there before, so he has asked Peter to find out about the country for him. Maggie has been to Zanada very often, so Peter telephones her. He knows a little about Zanada from books he has read.

PRACTICE POINT

Unsure	Sure
Zanada is rather rainy. **isn't it**?	He won't need warm clothes. **will he.**
• ··	⌐ .
Isn't it?	**Will he.**
= tell me if I am right or not.	= agree with me because I am obviously right.

3

1·2

YOUR AIM

Listen to Peter talking to Maggie. When is he asking her
if he is right or not? When is he expecting her to agree
with him? After each BLEEP, tick the appropriate box.

EXAMPLES

Peter: You've been to
Zanada, haven't you.
● . . .

Am I right?

1	2

Agree with me

1	2
✓	

Peter: Oh, yes, I
remember. You went
a couple of years ago,
didn't you?   ● . . .

Am I right?

1	2
	✓

Agree with me

1	2

EXERCISE

Am I right?

1	2	3	4	5	6

Agree with me

1	2	3	4	5	6

4

Which car did it?

SITUATION
There has been a
car crash just
outside the Tappa
Typewriter
Company offices.
It happened during
the lunch hour, and
several people were
looking out of the
window at the
time. A policeman
has come to the
Tappa Typewriter
offices. He is asking
the people who saw
the accident to
describe what
happened.

New words
apparently
I guess (informal) = I think
to smash
to smash into something

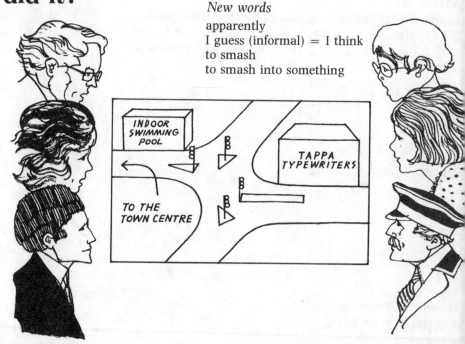

PRACTICE POINT

Active	*Passive*
The red car **hit** the blue one.	The red car **was hit** by the blue one.
Which car did it? = The red one.	Which car did it? = The blue one.

YOUR AIM
Listen to the people from Tappa Typewriters telling the
policeman about the accident. They have different ideas
about how the accident happened. Did the red car hit
the blue car? Or did the blue car hit the red car? After
each BLEEP, say which car apparently caused the accident.

💬 *You say:*

EXAMPLES

	You say:
1 *Policeman:* You saw the accident. Tell me what happened. *Woman:* The red car ran into the blue one. That's what happened! ● *Guide voice:* So the red one did it.	So the red one did it.
2 *Policeman:* I see. What did *you* see, sir? *Man:* As far as I could see, the red car was run into by the blue one. ● *Guide voice:* So the blue one did it.	So the blue one did it.

Who is the doer? Mike himself, or someone else?

to type
an account = a record of payments
a receipt

SITUATION
Mike Smith is talking to a difficult customer on the telephone. The customer, Mr Brown, keeps asking Mike a lot of questions; for example, 'Has my order been posted? Have the goods been sent off? Has my account been checked?'

PRACTICE POINT

Mike himself	Someone else
Mike says: I'm **typing** the letter. I **typed** the letter. I'll **type** the letter. etc.	Mike says: I'm **having** the letter typed. I **had** the letter typed. I'll **have** the letter typed. etc.

YOUR AIM
Listen to Mike. Does he say that he has done or will do the things *himself*? Or does he say that he has arranged or will arrange for *someone else* to do them? After each BLEEP, say 'Mike himself', or 'Someone else'.

You say:

EXAMPLES

1 *Mike:* Just a minute, Mr Brown . . . Yes . . . I've just checked the order book and . . . ● *Guide voice:* Mike himself.	Mike himself.
2 *Mike:* Yes, of course. Don't worry, I'll have them sent to your new address. ● *Guide voice:* Someone else.	Someone else.

6

1·5 📖

Is he asking a question?

SITUATION
Christine Daly and
Mike Smith are
talking about the
problem of storing
large quantities of
typewriters. Mike
keeps interrupting
Christine.

New words and phases
I haven't a clue (informal)
= I don't know
a warehouse

**PRACTICE
POINT**
The order of words
in a sentence
usually shows us
whether a question
is being asked
or not.

Questions	Not questions
Why **have you** written that?	I wonder why **you have** written that.
How much **will it** cost?	They'll tell me how much **it will** cost.
Where **is it**?	He hasn't a clue where **it is**.

YOUR AIM
Listen to Mike and Christine. When Mike interrupts, is he
asking Christine a new question, or is he finishing her
sentence for her? After each BLEEP, write ⑦ or ⊙ as
appropriate, as shown in the examples.

	📼	📖	⊙ not a question ⑦ a question
EXAMPLES	1 *Christine:* Oh sorry to bother you, Mike. I'm afraid I haven't a clue . . . *Mike:* What the time is. ● . . .	What	⊙
	2 *Christine:* Right. Anyway, now I'm here, I'm not sure . . . *Mike:* Why didn't you come and see me before? ● . . .	Why	⑦

EXERCISE

⊙ not a question

⑦ a question

1	What
2	How
3	How many
4	Where
5	How long
6	How much

7

Please could you tell me . . . ? (NATURAL SPEECH)

SITUATION

We recorded two telephone conversations in a busy
suburban company. They are both between two
executives and their secretaries. The first executive is
called Donald Mackay. He is Scottish and has a
Scottish accent. The second is called Tom Jackson. He is
English. Both the secretaries are English. We did not
record the whole of Donald's conversation. At the
beginning, he has just asked his secretary for some
information.

New words
an executive
a departure
an arrival
suburban

YOUR AIMS

1 First, listen to the conversation, to get a general
   understanding and to answer Question A. Don't stop
   the cassette while you listen.
2 Find out the answers to Question A. (They are in the
   key in the Guide.)
3 Listen again to understand the details and to
   answer questions B and C. Stop the cassette when you
   need to, and listen more than once if you want to.

QUESTIONS

A 1 How is Donald going to travel? Draw a circle round the appropriate picture.

2 How does Tom usually get home from work? Draw a circle round the appropriate picture.

The answers to Question A are in the key in the Guide.

B Now listen again to Donald talking to his secretary, and answer the questions below.

1 What times of departure and arrival does the secretary give to Donald?
Write the times below.

BARLOW (depart)	9·09				
LONDON↓ (arrive)					

2 Donald says: *'There aren't any fast ones, are there.'*
Is he asking a question or is he expecting her to agree? _____

3 Donald says: *'There's nothing quicker than that, is there.'*
Is he asking a question or is he expecting her to agree? _____

4 Donald says: *'That takes about half an hour to get in, doesn't it.'*
Is he asking a question or is he expecting her to agree? _____

5a) Write down the missing word which you hear: *'I'll take that _____ .'*

  b) Tick the right answer. What does he mean?
    I'll go on that train. ☐
    I'll make a note of the date today. ☐
    I'll write down that information. ☐

C Now listen again to Tom talking to his secretary and answer the questions below.

  1a) Write down the missing phrase which you hear: *'Yes, certainly. _____ .'*

  b) What does she mean? _____

  2a) Write down the missing word which you hear: *'I'm having my car _____ .'*

  b) Tick the right answer. What does he mean?
    I'm repairing the car. ☐
    Someone else is repairing the car. ☐
    Someone else is using the car. ☐
    I've had a car accident. ☐

  3 Tom says: *'That one doesn't stop at Audley End, does it.'*
  Is he asking a question or is he expecting her to agree? _____

PART TWO OPINIONS

Opinion or doubt?

New words
a sales model = a model for use by
  sales staff
major (adj.)
quite a job (informal) = rather a big
  task
a campaign = a programme of
  activities
pretty (adv.) (informal) = rather
to set up

SITUATION
Peter and Christine are talking about selling the latest
model of Tappa Typewriter. They are discussing the need
for advertising and for a visit to the larger European
cities.

PRACTICE POINT

An opinion	Uncertainty
．　●　．·	·　◝　．
I think we're ready to take a decision.	**I think** the papers are on my desk.
= this is my opinion.	= I'm not sure.

YOUR AIM

Listen to Christine and Peter. Listen to the way they say
'I think . . .' and 'He thinks . . .'. When do they mean
'This is an opinion'? When do they mean 'This is
uncertain'? After each BLEEP, tick the appropriate box.

EXAMPLES

1 *Christine*: I think we'd better start . . . . . .

1	2
✓	

2 *Christine*: Have you heard from Harry?
Peter: Oh, he's working really hard at the moment but
he thinks the sales model'll be ready on time. . . .

1	2
	✓

EXERCISE

1	2	3	4	5	6

1	2	3	4	5	6

Did they see it themselves, or not?

New words
terribly (informal) = very,
wreckage
to swerve
to collapse

SITUATION
Maggie, Peter, Christine, Mike, Joanna and some other friends are having a drink together. They are talking about an accident at a motor race the previous day.

PRACTICE POINT

I saw it	*I did not see it*
The track **seemed** to be wet. The track **appeared** to be wet.	The track was wet, **apparently**. **Apparently**, the track was wet. **It seems** the track was wet.
= This is the speaker's opinion. He or she saw the track.	= This is someone else's opinion. The speaker did not see the track.

YOUR AIM

Listen to the group of friends talking about the car accident. Which of them saw the accident? After each BLEEP, write 'Yes' or 'No' in the appropriate places.

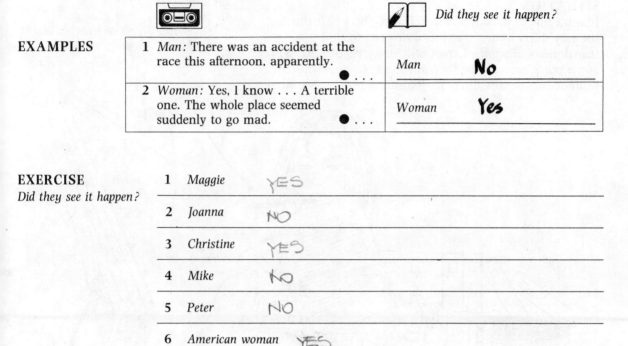

Did they see it happen?

EXAMPLES		
1 *Man:* There was an accident at the race this afternoon, apparently. ● ...	Man	**No**
2 *Woman:* Yes, I know ... A terrible one. The whole place seemed suddenly to go mad. ● ...	Woman	**Yes**

EXERCISE

Did they see it happen?

1	Maggie	YES
2	Joanna	NO
3	Christine	YES
4	Mike	NO
5	Peter	NO
6	American woman	YES

Is it logical or is it nonsense?

New words
research (noun)
logical
illogical
a shortage
an import
to import
USSR = the Union of Soviet Socialist
Republics

SITUATION
Joanna has to do some research into the USSR during
the last thirty years. She has managed to find
translations of some of the USSR news reports. However,
some parts are very badly translated; some of the
sentences are quite illogical. Joanna is reading aloud.

PRACTICE POINT	Logical	Illogical
	Situation: John hasn't eaten anything for days. *Result:*　He **must be** feeling very hungry. 　*or* He, is, **therefore**, feeling very hungry. 　*or* **So**, he's feeling very hungry.	*Situation:* John has had three big meals today. *Result:*　He **must be** feeling hungry after so much food. 　*or* He is, **therefore**, feeling very hungry. 　*or* **So**, he's feeling rather hungry now.
	The second sentences express a *logical* result of the situation given in the first sentence.	The second sentences are connected *illogically* to the first sentence. They are nonsense.

YOUR AIM

Listen to Joanna reading parts of the translated scripts.
Is what she reads logical, or is it illogical? After each
BLEEP, tick the appropriate box.

EXAMPLES

1 *Joanna:* The last
harvest was very bad
and so there is now
plenty of food.
● . . .

Logical

1	2

Illogical

1 ✔	2

2 *Joanna:* The last
harvest was very bad.
The people must now
be short of food.
● . . .

Logical

1	2 ✔

Illogical

1	2

EXERCISE

Logical

1	2 ✓	3 ✓	4

Illogical

1 ✓	2	3	4 ✓

Is someone unable to do it now? Or is it impossible that someone did it in the past?

New words
to meet an order = to supply the
  goods ordered
a bit = rather
I bet (informal) = I am sure
to look into = to find out about
to make it (informal) = to arrive
  in time

SITUATION
Mike and Christine are checking through recent orders
and accounts together. Mike is asking Christine about
some of them.

PRACTICE POINT

Impossible now	*Apparently impossible in the past*
We **can't meet** this order.	We **can't have met** this order.
= We are unable to meet this order.	= It seems impossible to me that we met this order.

YOUR AIM
Listen to Mike and Christine. In her answers to Mike's
questions, does Christine speak of inability or past
impossibility? After each BLEEP, tick the appropriate box.

2·4

EXAMPLES

Mike: Where's Peter? *Christine:* Oh, he can't make it after all. ● ...	*Unable (now)* 1 ✓ 2 *Impossible (past)* 1 2

Mike: OK. Well, never mind. Now where's the order book? *Christine:* Oh dear, I'm afraid they can't've sent it up. But don't worry. I'll go and get it. ● ...	*Unable (now)* 1 2 *Impossible (past)* 1 2 ✓

EXERCISE

Unable (now) | 1 | 2 | 3 | 4 | 5 | 6 |

Impossible (past) | 1 | 2 | 3 | 4 | 5 | 6 |

What does it mean?

New words
a snack bar
a sieve (pronounced 'siv')

SITUATION

Maggie and a friend of hers, Graham, are meeting for lunch. Maggie arrives a little late and she apologises to Graham. Then they carry on talking.

PRACTICE POINT

Sometimes you may hear people use a word or phrase which you don't know. This can happen in your own language, but more often it happens in a foreign language. You can often guess the meaning of the word or phrase by listening carefully to everything else that the person is saying. In this exercise you are going to practise this kind of guessing. It is a very useful skill.

YOUR AIM

First, just listen to Maggie and Graham. Then you will hear them again. After each BLEEP, you will hear a question about a phrase used by Maggie or Graham. Write the meaning of the phrase in the space provided. Each of the phrases has something to do with *remembering* or *forgetting*.

EXAMPLE

 NOTE: *This example is not on the cassette.*

| *Question* What do you think 'Let bygones be bygones' means? After the BLEEP, write your answer in the Workbook. | She was always thinking about when she used to live in India; she couldn't understand when I told her she should look to the future and let bygones be bygones. She just ignored me and carried on dreaming. ● . . . | *Answer* It means *forget about the past* |

EXERCISE

Answers
1 It means

2 It means

3 It means

4 It means

Who does he think they are? (NATURAL SPEECH)

SITUATION

Caroline showed three pictures to her neighbour, John, and asked him to guess who the people in the pictures were or what kinds of job they had. John is a part-time gardener in London, and in the evenings he plays the drums in a jazz group. He has a suburban London accent. He feels rather unsure of himself when he is talking into a tape recorder.

New words
a gangster
flashy
a hobby
a forefather

YOUR AIMS

1 First, listen once to John talking about the pictures, to get a general understanding of what he said. Don't stop the cassette while you listen. Then answer Question A.
2 Find out the answers to Question A. (They are in the key in the Guide.)
3 Listen again to understand the details and to answer Questions B, C and D. Stop the cassette when you need to, and listen more than once if you want to.

QUESTIONS

A Here are four pictures. John is talking about three of them. Which is the first picture he talks about? Which is the second? Which is the third? Write '1st', '2nd', '3rd' under the appropriate pictures.

2

3

4

The answers to Question A are in the key in the Guide.

20

B   Now listen again to John talking about the first picture and answer the questions below:

1a) Write down the missing word which you hear: *'I - I think this fellow is um is a gangster from*

    the _____ .'

  b) Tick the right answer. What does John mean?
  He's a gangster aged between 30 and 40. □
  He was a gangster between 1930 and 1940. □
  He's a gangster from a particular part of the USA. □

2   John says *'I - I think this fellow is um is a gangster . . .'*
  Is he expressing his opinion or is he expressing doubt? _____

3a) Write down the missing word which you hear:

    'I'm sure it is by the _____ of his clothes.'

  b) What does he mean?
  He's sure because of the colour   □ of his clothes.
                          cleanness   □
                          style   □

4   John thinks this is a photograph of a man called Baby-faced Nelson, a member of the Mafia.
  Write down FOUR of the reasons why John thinks this.
  Because _____

  Because _____

  Because _____

  Because _____

C   Now listen again to John talking about the second picture, and answer the questions below:
  1   Is this the first time John has seen this picture? _____

  2   Has he discussed this picture with anyone else? _____

      If so, who? _____
  3   John says, *'I think he's writing music.'*
      Is he expressing his opinion or is he expressing doubt? _____

D   Now listen again to John talking about the third picture, and answer the questions below:
  1a) Write down the missing phrase that you hear. (Each blank stands for one word.)

    'Well, he _____ _____ _____ _____ _____ of what my forefathers were supposed to look like.'

  b) What does John mean? _____
  2   John says this man looks 'miserable'. What does he mean?
  He looks poor. □
             sad. □
             unpleasant. □
  3   Why wouldn't John like him as a next-door neighbour?
  He would probably make a lot of noise. □
  He would always be knocking at the door. □
  He would be unfriendly. □

PART THREE   LIKES AND DISLIKES

What was that word?

New words
to sneeze
an echo
an aspirin
whisky
to long for = want very much

SITUATION
Maggie has got a bad cold. She is feeling miserable.
She is trying to explain what she wants. Each time she
comes to the most important part of her sentence, she
sneezes loudly so that a word is lost.

PRACTICE POINT Using echo questions to ask someone to repeat something

			Echo question
I love having	ATCHOO!		I'm sorry? You love having what?
I hate being	ATCHOO!		I'm sorry? You hate being what?
I'd love a	ATCHOO!		I'm sorry? You'd love a what?

YOUR AIM
Listen to Maggie. After each BLEEP, ask her to repeat
what she has just said, by asking an echo question.

📼 💬 *You say:*

EXAMPLE

Maggie: I'd like a – ATCHOO! ●	I'm sorry? You'd like a what?
Guide voice: I'm sorry? You'd like a what?	*You'd rather what?*

Tell me about her, or tell me what she likes

New words
a typist

SITUATION
Peter is chatting on the phone to Maggie. They are talking about various women, including Maggie's new secretary and the typist.

PRACTICE POINT

Describe her	What does she like?
What's (What **is**) she like?	What **does** she like?
What'll she **be** like?	What'll she like?
What would she **be** like?	What **would** she like?
What **was** she like? etc.	What **did** she like? etc.

YOUR AIM

Listen carefully to Peter. Does he want to know about
the woman herself? Or does he want to know what she
likes? After each BLEEP, tick the appropriate box.

EXAMPLES

1 *Peter:* Hello. Just
   waiting for the
   typist. She's coming
   back today. I wonder
   what she'll be like
   after her illness. ● . . .

   She herself | 1 ✓ | 2 |

   What she likes | 1 | 2 |

2 *Peter:* I don't know.
   What do *you* think
   she'd like? ● . . .

   She herself | 1 | 2 |

   What she likes | 1 | 2 ✓ |

EXERCISE

She herself | 1 | 2 | 3 | 4 | 5 | 6 |

What she likes | 1 | 2 | 3 | 4 | 5 | 6 |

Is she interested or not?

New words
jazz (noun)
night-life = activities at night (e.g. in
    restaurants)
an 'X' film = a film which may be
    seen by adults only
a Western = a film about cowboys,
    etc. in the western United States

SITUATION
Peter is phoning Joanna to ask her to go to the cinema
with him.

PRACTICE POINT

Interested, enthusiastic	Uninterested, unenthusiastic
◟	◝
Oh!	Oh!

YOUR AIM
Listen to Peter and Joanna. Listen, especially, to the way
Joanna says 'Oh'. Is she interested and enthusiastic about
what Peter tells her, or not? After each BLEEP, draw
the appropriate mouth.

EXAMPLES

1 *Peter:* Hello? Joanna? Oh, hello. I was wondering if you'd like to go out this evening. *Joanna:* Oh ●...	☺
2 *Peter:* I was thinking about a jazz concert ... *Joanna:* Oh ●...	☹

EXERCISE

1   2   3   4   5   6

Has he finished speaking?

New words
to interview
lemonade

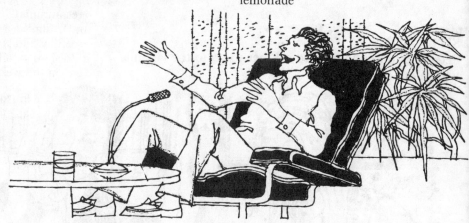

SITUATION
You are
interviewing an
American filmstar
for a television
programme. He is
telling you about
his likes and
dislikes.

PRACTICE POINT

He wants to add something	He has finished his sentence
· · · ⌣	· · · · ⌣
I like coffee and **tea** . . .	I like coffee and **tea**.

YOUR AIM
Listen to the American filmstar. When he hesitates, is he
going to add something more? Or has he finished what
he wants to say? You will hear a BLEEP when he
hesitates. If you think he wants to add something, say
'Yes?'. If you think he has finished, say 'I see'.

💬 *You say:*

EXAMPLES

1 *American:* W-e-ell, I just love rice and fish . . . ● *Guide voice:* Yes?	Yes?
2 *American:* Well, as I was saying, I just love rice and fish and tomato sauce. ● *Guide voice:* I see.	I see.

Is this surprising or not?

New words
a resort = a holiday place
a contrast
room-staff = hotel staff who provide
  services in the bedrooms
awful (informal) = very bad

SITUATION
Maggie is abroad visiting a new holiday resort on
business. Graham is telephoning her to find out how
she is getting on. The telephone line is bad, so
Maggie's words are sometimes not clear.

PRACTICE POINT

But . . . (this is surprising)	And . . . (this is not surprising)
The hotel is cheap, **but** it is comfortable. The hotel is cheap **and yet** it is comfortable. **Although** the hotel is cheap, it is comfortable. The hotel is cheap. **However**, it is comfortable.	The hotel is uncomfortable **and** it is noisy (**too**). The hotel is uncomfortable (**and**), **what is more**, it is noisy. The hotel is uncomfortable. **Also**, it is noisy. The hotel is uncomfortable (**and**), **moreover**, it is noisy. **Not only** is the hotel uncomfortable **but** it is noisy (**too**).
But, **and yet**, **although** and **however** express a contrast between two situations, ideas, etc.	**And**, **too**, **what is more**, **also**, **moreover** and **not only . . . but . . . too/also** express a similarity between two situations, ideas, etc.

3·5

YOUR AIM

Listen to Maggie and Graham. The bad telephone line
makes it impossible to hear everything Maggie says.
After each BLEEP, tick the words which you think
should end Maggie's sentence.

EXAMPLES

1 *Graham:* Hello? Maggie? What's the hotel like? Is it comfortable? *Maggie:* Well, yes; on the whole it's very comfortable but the food . . . (*crackle*) ● . . .	*a)* isn't good ✓ *b)* is very good	2 *Graham:* And what about the people? Nice? *Maggie:* Oh, yes. The room-staff are really nice and friendly and, what is more, the waiters . . . (*crackle*) ● . . .	*a)* are unhelpful *b)* are excellent ✓

EXERCISE

a) very sweet

b) rather noisy

2 *a)* very clean

b) very dirty

3 *a)* is clean

b) is dirty, too

4 *a)* it's quite pleasant enough

b) it's very unpleasant

5 *a)* we arrived on time

b) we arrived late, too

What do they like eating? (NATURAL SPEECH)

SITUATION

Ann Harding interviewed five people about their eating habits: what they like and what they do not like, and what kinds of food they usually have. She recorded their answers, and here are parts of the recording.

YOUR AIMS

1 First, listen once to the five speakers, to get a general understanding of what they said. Do not stop the cassette while you listen. Answer Question A.
2 Listen again to understand the details and to answer Questions B to F. Stop the cassette when you need to, and listen more than once if you want to.

New words

to get carried away with = to become excited about

convenience foods = foods which are already partly cooked when they are sold, and which are therefore quick and easy to prepare

steak and kidney pie

pastry

meat

fish-fingers

corned beef (colloquial: corn beef) = tinned beef

baked beans = tinned beans with tomato sauce

QUESTIONS

A The five people spoke to Ann Harding in this order:
   1 Susan Johns   2 Tony Blakemore   3 Gareth Jones   4 Bob Giddens
   5 Mike Smith

Guess who's who and write the name under each photograph.

A record
producer

A student

A building
maintenance
man

A schoolboy

An executive

_____   _____   _____   _____   _____

B Now listen to Susan Johns again and answer the questions below:
   1a) Write down the missing word which you hear: '*I have a very* _____ *stomach.*'
   b) Tick the right answer. What does she mean?
       She's got a very strong ☐ stomach.
                      unusual ☐
                      weak ☐

2a) 'Eating out' means here:
    Having a picnic. ☐
          a meal at home. ☐
          a meal at a restaurant. ☐

b) 'Eating in' means here:
    Having a meal at home. ☐
          a meal at a friend's house. ☐
          a meal at a restaurant. ☐

c) Which does Susan Johns prefer: the atmosphere of 'eating out' or 'eating in'? _____

C Now listen to Tony Blakemore again and answer the questions below:

1   What sort of meat do he and his wife usually eat? _____
2   Listen carefully to the list of foods they usually eat.

Is the list complete? _____

D Now listen to Gareth Jones again and answer the questions below:

1   Do Gareth and his mother always eat convenience foods? _____
2   Listen carefully to the list of convenience foods.

Is the list complete? _____

E Now listen to Bob Giddens again and answer the questions below:

1a) Write down the missing word which you hear: *'My favourite dish is roast pork and er with*

_____ *of erm apple sauce.'*

b) What do you think the word means? _____ _____

2a) Write down the missing word which you hear:

'I think that's what _____ *roast pork for me.'*
b) Bob means here:
    I think roast pork and apple sauce together is best. ☐
    roast pork without apple sauce is best. ☐
    I like apple sauce better than roast pork. ☐
c) Is Bob expressing his opinion here or is he expressing doubt? _____

3a) Write down the missing word which you hear:

'One day you could _____ *something.'*
b) Bob means here:
    You could buy   ☐ something.
            dislike   ☐
            want   ☐
c) Does the pronoun 'you' here mean Ann Harding or people in general? _____

4   What do you think *'you've gone off (of) it'* means?
    You no longer dislike it. ☐
    You no longer like it. ☐
    You still like it.   ☐

F Now listen to Mike Smith again and answer the questions below:

1a) Write down the missing word which you hear:

'I'm also quite _____ *to beans.'*

b) Does he like beans? _____

PART FOUR   APPROVAL AND DISAPPROVAL

Is Mike unsure,
or is he annoyed?

New words
indignant
honestly! = really! (usually
   suggesting disapproval)
to book

SITUATION
Mike and Christine are in the office. They are talking
about a variety of things.

PRACTICE POINT

Unsure	*Indignant*
· ⌒ ·	• ⌒ •
He **might** have come.	He **might** have come.
= the speaker is not sure if he came.	= the speaker is indignant because he did not come.

YOUR AIM
Listen to Mike. When is he unsure? When is he
indignant? After each BLEEP, tick the appropriate box.

4·1

EXAMPLES

1 *Christine:* Is Peter coming?
Mike: He said he was, but he might have been called away. ● . . .

2 *Christine:* Oh yes, that's right. He's got an important customer to see this afternoon.
Mike: He might have mentioned it to me. ● . . .

EXERCISE

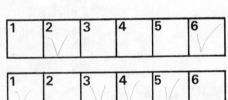

How do you say you're sorry?

New words
intense

SITUATION

Peter is in bed. He is having a very bad dream. He is at a party. Everything seems to be going wrong and each time it is Peter's fault. He keeps on apologising.

PRACTICE POINT

Normal	*Intense*
I'm sorry Sorry (informal) }(+ explanation) So sorry (informal)	I'm *so* sorry I'm terribly sorry (informal) }(+ explanation) I'm extremely sorry

YOUR AIM

Listen to Peter apologising. Is he apologising for something serious? Or is he apologising for something fairly unimportant? After each BLEEP, say 'Something serious', or 'Something unimportant'.

You say:

EXAMPLES

	You say:
1 *Peter:* Sorry about the lamp. ● *Guide voice:* Something unimportant.	Something unimportant.
2 *Peter:* I'm *so* sorry about the carpet. I can't think how I managed to do it. ● *Guide voice:* Something serious.	Something serious.

35

Did it happen or not?

SITUATION
Joanna is talking on the telephone to Peter, who is
staying with friends for the weekend. Joanna and Peter
are talking about what they have been doing.

PRACTICE POINT

It happened	It did not happen
· ⌐ · ⌐ ·	· · · ⌐
I **thought** you'd see them.	I **thought** you'd see them.
· ⌐ · ⌐ · ·	· · · · ⌐ ·
I **thought** you'd enjoy yourself.	I **thought** you'd enjoy yourself.
= You saw them, as I expected. You are enjoying yourself, as I expected.	= But you did not see them. But you are not enjoying yourself.

4·3

YOUR AIM
Listen to Joanna. Did things happen as she expected
they would? Or did they not happen? After each
BLEEP, answer the question in the Workbook.
Just write 'Yes' or 'No'.

EXAMPLES

1 *Joanna:* Hello. Are you having a good time? . . . *Joanna:* I thought you'd be having a lovely time. ● . . .	*Question* Is Peter having a lovely time? *Answer* **No**
2 *Joanna:* I thought it would probably rain.. ● . . .	*Question* Has it been raining? *Answer* **Yes**

EXERCISE

1 *Question* Did they all turn up to the party?

Answer

2 *Question* Did she get drunk?

Answer

3 *Question* Did she apologise?

Answer

4 *Question* Did Peter's brother telephone?

Answer

5 *Question* Had Peter made a mistake?

Answer

6 *Question* Is Peter coming over this evening?

Answer

Wish or regret?

New words
to book in = to report one's arrival
 at a hotel desk, etc.
an essay

SITUATION

It is 2 o'clock in the morning. Everyone is in bed,
dreaming. Sometimes they are dreaming and hoping
about the future. Sometimes they are dreaming about
the past and wishing it had been different.

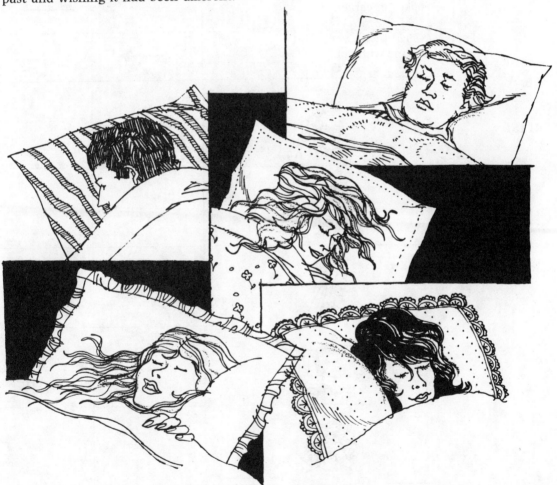

PRACTICE POINT

A wish for the future	*A regret about the past*
I wish he'd (he **would**) **write** to me.	I wish he'd (he **had**) **written** to me.
(= perhaps he will)	(= but he did not)

4·4

YOUR AIM
Listen to these people talking in their sleep. Are they
hoping for something in the future? Or are they sorry
about something in the past? After each BLEEP, draw
an arrow like this ⟶ for hopes about the future, and
like this ⟵ for regrets about the past, by the
picture.

EXAMPLES

	Future	Past
1 *Maggie:* I wish you'd booked in earlier. ● . . .		⟵
2 *Joanna:* I wish you'd take me with you. ● . . .	⟶	

EXERCISE

		Future	Past
1			⟵
2		⟶	
3			⟵
4			⟵
5		⟶	
6		⟶	

Not at all, or only in special cases?

New words
odd = strange
to go out with (informal)

SITUATION
Joanna is talking to Peter on the telephone. They are planning to go out with Mary, the girl who shares a room with Joanna.

PRACTICE POINT

Not at all	*Only if it is a special case*
. • • • \..	. • • • ~.
She won't write to **anyone**.	She won't write to **anyone**.
= She will write to no one at all.	= She will write *only* to the people she *chooses* to write to.

4·5

Listen to Joanna. When does she mean 'Not at all'?
When does she mean 'Only in special cases'? After each
BLEEP, tick the appropriate box.

EXAMPLES

1 *Joanna*: Who? Mary?
She doesn't go out
with *anyone*, you
know. ● . . .

Not at all | 1 | 2 |

Only if . . . | 1 ✓ | 2 |

2 *Joanna*: No. She told
me. She doesn't like
anybody. ● . . .

Not at all | 1 | 2 ✓ |

Only if . . . | 1 | 2 |

EXERCISE

Not at all | 1 | 2 | 3 | 4 | 5 | 6 |

Only if . . . | 1 | 2 | 3 | 4 | 5 | 6 |

Do they approve of the bus service? (NATURAL SPEECH)

New words
a timetable

SITUATION
Ann Harding asked three colleagues what they thought about the bus service in their town. They were: Bob Giddens, a building maintenance man, Brenda Smith, a secretary, and Pam Campbell, a sales assistant. Ann recorded part of their answers.

YOUR AIMS
1 First, listen once to the three speakers, to get a general understanding of what they said. Do not stop the cassette while you listen. Answer Question A.
2 Listen again, to understand the details and to answer Questions B–D. Stop the cassette when you need to, and listen more than once if you want to.

QUESTIONS

A Complete the form with a ✔ for 'Yes' and a ✗ for 'No'.

	Bob Giddens	Brenda Smith	Pam Campbell
Approves of the bus service			
Usually travels to work by bus			

B Now listen to Bob Giddens again and answer the questions below:

1a) Write down the missing word which you hear: *'because the bus service is so* _____.'

b) Tick the right box. What does he mean?
    The bus service is very good. ☐
    rather good. ☐
    very bad. ☒

2 Which diagram best illustrates the bus service
  a) as it is now?
  b) as Bob thinks it should be?
Write the appropriate description under the matching diagram.

- - - = bus routes

_____   _____   _____

3 Bob says, *'I think they could do more —'.*
Is he expressing his opinion or is he expressing doubt?

4 Bob says, *'You've got to go to the town centre.'*
Does 'you' here mean Ann Harding or people in general?

C Listen to Brenda Smith again and answer the questions below:

1*a)* Write down the missing word which you hear:

  'I think the bus service is _____ .'
 b) She means: The bus service is very bad. ☒
             not too bad. ☐
             rather good. ☐

2 Brenda says, *'They could turn up for one thing.'*

 a) Who or what are 'they'? _____
 b) What other word could you use instead of 'turn up'? _____

3 Which does Brenda say? 'Oh well, five minutes to eight'. ☐
            too late'. ☐
            to wait'. ☒

D Listen to Pam Campbell again and answer the questions below:

1 Pam usually comes to work by bus. ☐
          in someone else's car. ☐
          in her own car. ☐

2 Pam says, *'I think there should be some way —'*
Is she expressing her opinion or is she expressing doubt? _____

PART FIVE   GETTING THINGS DONE

Who is going to do it?

New words
what on earth . . .? = a forceful
  way of saying 'what . . .?
under the circumstances
to draft = to plan the wording

SITUATION
It is nine o'clock in the morning. Christine is talking to
Mike about the things that need to be done today.

PRACTICE POINT

Do it!	I will do it
I'd (I **would**) write that letter now (if I were you).	I'll (I **will**) write that letter now.
= I advise *you* to write it.	= *I* am going to write it.

YOUR AIM
Listen to Mike and Christine talking. When is Mike
advising Christine to do something? When is he going to
do something himself? After each BLEEP, take Christine's
part and say 'OK, I will' or 'Oh, will you! Good'.

You say:

EXAMPLES

1 *Christine:* What on earth am I going to do with all these, Mike? *Mike:* Oh, I'll move them. ● *Guide voice:* Oh, will you! Good.	Oh, will you! Good.
2 *Christine:* And what about this letter? *Mike:* I think I'd throw it away now. ● *Guide voice:* OK, I will.	OK, I will.

What is she talking about?

New words
a topic
to excuse
make sure! = don't fail to
a queue

SITUATION
Maggie is talking to Joanna on the telephone. She is giving her advice on various topics.

PRACTICE POINT
Sometimes you may listen to people talking and have no idea what they are talking about. But if you keep listening carefully, you may discover what their topic is.

YOUR AIM
Listen to Maggie talking to Joanna. What is Maggie advising her about? After each BLEEP, write or draw your answer in the Workbook.

EXAMPLE

NOTE: *This example is not on the cassette.*

Yes, I know. It's like me. I could see perfectly well until I was about twenty. Then things started getting a bit difficult at the cinema and places like that. But anyway, you be sure to follow his advice. If he says 'Wear them for reading', you should wear them.

She's talking about
glasses/spectacles

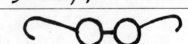

EXERCISE

1   She's talking about _____

2   She's talking about _____

3   She's talking about _____

4   She's talking about _____

What is she trying to say?

New words
tactful
tentative(ly)
goodness! (informal)

SITUATION
Joanna is talking to Peter on the telephone. Part of the
time she wants to ask him for various favours, and part
of the time she wants to give him some advice. She is
trying to be very tactful all the time.

PRACTICE POINT
A very usual way of being tactful in English is to
approach a subject in an indirect, tentative way.

Direct Approach	Tentative Approach
1 *Making a request* Could you buy me a newspaper, please?	1 *Making a request* Will you be passing the paper shop when you go shopping? . . . (*Why? What d'you want?* Well, could you buy me a newspaper?)
2 *Giving advice* You ought to work harder.	2 *Giving advice* I hope you don't mind my saying this, but . . . (*What? What's the matter?* I really think you ought to work harder.)

YOUR AIM

Listen to Joanna. Is she going to ask a favour? Or is she
going to give some advice? After each BLEEP, tick the
appropriate box.

EXAMPLES

1 *Joanna:* Oh hello,
it's Joanna here.
Look, will you be
passing the Post
Office on your way
back to lunch? ● ...

Asking a favour

1	2
✓	

2 *Joanna:* Yes. I see.
Well, look, if you
don't mind my
saying so . . . ● ...

Giving advice

1	2
	✓

EXERCISE

Asking a favour

1	2	3	4	5	6

Giving advice

1	2	3	4	5	6

Is she asking why?
Or is she making a suggestion?

New words
a day off

SITUATION
Joanna is talking to Peter on the phone. She is trying to persuade him to join her and some friends on a trip to the seaside.

PRACTICE POINT

Tell me why . . .	*I suggest . . .*
Why **won't** you speak to him?	Why **don't** you speak to him?
= Why do you refuse to speak to him?	= I suggest you speak to him.

YOUR AIM
Listen to Joanna. When is she asking for a reason? When is she making a suggestion? After each BLEEP, tick the appropriate box.

5·4

EXAMPLES

Joanna: Why won't you come with us tomorrow? ● . . .

Why?

| 1 ✔ | 2 |

I suggest . . .

| 1 | 2 |

Joanna: Well, why don't you ask him for a day off? ● . . .

Why?

| 1 | 2 |

I suggest . . .

| 1 | 2 ✔ |

EXERCISE

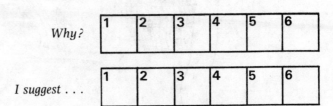

Why?

| 1 | 2 | 3 | 4 | 5 | 6 |

I suggest . . .

| 1 | 2 | 3 | 4 | 5 | 6 |

Which is she to do?

New words
a brochure
a receptionist
to contact
a representative
to book someone in = reserve a
  room for

SITUATION
Maggie Parkin is telling her secretary, Pat, various
things that she wants Pat to do. Pat is making notes.

PRACTICE POINT

Send him a letter **rather than** a telegram.	Send him a letter, **or rather** a telegram.
= send him a letter.	= send him a telegram (I've changed my mind).

YOUR AIM
Listen to Maggie. What exactly does she want Pat to do?
After each BLEEP, complete Pat's notes on what she
has to do.

EXAMPLES

1 *Pat:* There's another letter from Mr Smith today, Miss Parkin. *Maggie:* Oh Lord, yes. Look, could you send him a Spanish brochure . . . or rather send him ten of the things. ● . . .	*Send Mr Smith ten Spanish brochures*
2 *Pat:* Yes, right, I'll do that. *Maggie:* And send them *first* class rather than second. ● . . .	*Send them first class*

EXERCISE

1 *Arrange something with* _____

2 _____ *the Managers.*

3 *Or the* _____

4 *Book a room for* _____

5 *Arrange travel by* _____

Who's going to do what? (NATURAL SPEECH)

SITUATION
We recorded three telephone conversations in a large company in London. Three young executives rang their secretaries. You will hear Jan talking to Carol, Annie talking to Wendy and Chris talking to Elisabeth. You will hear only part of each conversation.

YOUR AIMS
1 First, just listen to the three conversations to get a general understanding. Do not stop the cassette while you listen.
2 Listen again to understand the details and to answer the questions. Stop the cassette when you need to, and listen more than once if you want to.

New words
a retained adviser = someone who receives a regular fee in return for giving advice whenever it is needed
to draw up a contract
a formula
a couple = two
stationery
hang on (informal) = wait a moment
an invoice

QUESTIONS

A Listen to Jan talking to Carol and then answer the questions below:
1 Jan says, *'I think that probably the best thing . . . .'*
  a) Is she expressing her opinion or is she expressing doubt? _____
  b) We can't hear the end of her sentence. What sort of thing is she going to say? Tick the right answer.
    She's going to ask Carol to do something. ☐
              give Carol some advice. ☐

2a) Write down the missing word which you hear: *'Why _____ you ask Meg . . . ?'*
  b) Is this a question or a suggestion? _____

3a) What does Jan say? *' _____ , yes, ask Meg.'*
  b) What does Jan mean?
    She will ask Meg herself. ☐
    She wants Carol to ask Meg. ☐

4 Jan says, *'I think it's just a question of asking . . . .'*
  Is she expressing her opinion or is she expressing doubt? _____

5a) What does Jan say? *' _____ do a note.'*
  b) What does Jan mean?
    She will do a note herself. ☐
    She wants Carol to do a note. ☐

B Listen to Annie talking to Wendy and then answer the questions below:
1 Annie says *'I wonder if you could do 10 copies of them'.*

  What does Annie want 10 copies of? _____

2a) What does Annie say? *' _____ go to the machine downstairs.'*
  b) What does she mean?
    She will go to the machine herself. ☐
    She wants Wendy to go to the machine. ☐

3a) Write down the missing word which you hear: ' _____ of people'
 b) What does she mean?
The people who use the machine have made it untidy. ☐
There are lots of people wanting to use the machine. ☐
The machine is blocked and out of order. ☐

4 Annie says, 'If you're going to the stationery office —'
What sort of thing is she going to say next?
She's going to ask Wendy to do something. ☐
                  give Wendy some advice. ☐

C Listen to Chris talking to Elisabeth and then answer the questions below:
 1a) Write down the missing phrase which you hear: 'could you please _____ _____
a company cheque.'
 b) What does Chris mean?
He wants Elisabeth to look at ☐ a cheque.
                  write ☐
                  post ☐

2 Here is a cheque. In the spaces provided, write down the name and amount of money
which you hear:

3 Chris thinks one ☐ cheque(s) would be better.
          two ☐

GUIDE

1·1
Who are they
talking about? (*page 1*)

PRACTICE POINT

1 Impersonal 'you' occurs a great deal in conversation. It is used in informal language only, and means the same as 'one', used in more formal language, and 'people', used in neutral language.

> People usually enjoy a good joke. (neutral)
> One usually enjoys a good joke. (formal)
> You usually enjoy a good joke. (informal)

2 Impersonal 'you' does not necessarily include the person or people being addressed.

> A hundred years ago, you couldn't travel very comfortably.

3 The context usually helps one to infer which meaning of 'you' is intended. When this is not possible, English speakers usually ask: 'Do you mean *me*, or people in general?'

DOING THE EXERCISE

1 The context makes the meaning of each 'you' clear.

2 If there are two or more 'you's' between BLEEPS, they are *all* personal or *all* impersonal.

NOTE

'Your' and 'yourself' can similarly have an impersonal meaning.

TAPESCRIPT OF EXERCISE

Examples. First, just listen to Joanna and Peter. When does the word 'you' refer to the other person and when does it refer to people in general?

Joanna: I didn't expect to see you back so soon.
    ● ...

Peter: (laughing slightly) Nor did I! I wanted to stay longer, but you're not allowed to stay more than two weeks. ● ...

Now do the exercise. After each BLEEP, tick the appropriate box in the Workbook.

Joanna: That island you visited sounds great ...
    ● ... but did you really have to travel everywhere by horse and cart? ● ...
Peter: Yep. That's right. Cars aren't allowed. You're not even allowed to use a motorbike! ● ...
Joanna: Ooh! Sounds fantastic! You must've hated coming back. ● ...
Peter: Yeah (*slightly rueful laugh*) but I suppose you generally feel like that after a holiday, don't you.
    ● ...
Joanna: Mm. Suppose so. What was the food like?
Peter: Great! Really superb! There was plenty to choose from and you couldn't eat it all. There was so much ... ● ...

KEY

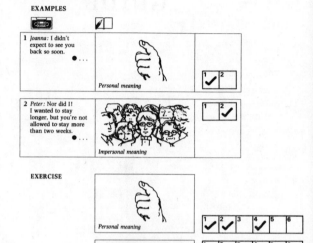

EXAMPLES

EXERCISE

FOR THE TEACHER: FURTHER WORK

You can ask students to look for examples of 'you' and 'one' in interviews heard on the radio or read in newspapers.

1·2
Is he asking a question, or does he just want her to agree? (*page* 3)

SITUATION
Zanada is an imaginary country.

PRACTICE POINT
1 Someone who uses either kind of question tag usually expects some sort of reply.

2 In writing, both kinds of tag questions are usually punctuated with a question mark. However, for the falling-tone tag, an exclamation mark is sometimes used or (as here) a full-stop.

NOTE
1 *Agreeing with tag questions*

A Montreal is on an island, isn't it?	B Yes, it is. (You're right.)
A It isn't warm today, is it.	B No, it isn't (I agree with you.)

2 *Disagreeing with tag questions*

A Montreal is near the sea, isn't it?	B (Well,) actually, it isn't. (It's quite far from the sea.)
A It isn't raining at the moment, is it.	B (Well,) actually, it is. (In fact, it's raining quite hard.)

'Actually' is used to soften one's disagreement, making it more tactful.

TAPESCRIPT OF EXERCISE
Examples. First, just listen to Peter. When is he asking if he is right or not? When is he asking Maggie to agree with him?

Peter: You've been to Zanada, haven't you. ● . . .
Peter: Oh yes, I remember. You went a couple of

years ago, didn't you? ● . . .
Now do the exercise. After each BLEEP, tick the appropriate box in the Workbook.

Peter: Now, let's see . . . It's er, it's a mainly

agricultural country, isn't it. ● . . .
Peter: Well yes, I know, but there's not much

industry once you've left the coast, is there? ● . . .

Peter: I see . . . Mm, so the North would be the

best place to go to, wouldn't it. ● . . .
Peter: Yeah. Mind you, I should think the South is

very beautiful, isn't it. ● . . .
Peter: (*laughs*) Yeah. That's right. Oh and what about

transport? It'd be better to hire a car, wouldn't it?
● . . .
Peter: Really? That's cheap. It costs that much a day

here, doesn't it. ● . . .
Peter: Yeah, well that's fine, Maggie. Thanks a lot. Bye.

KEY
EXAMPLES

| 1 *Peter:* You've been to Zanada, haven't you. ● . . . | *Am I right?* | 1 | 2 |
| | *Agree with me* | 1 ✓ | 2 |

| 2 *Peter:* Oh, yes, I remember. You went a couple of years ago, didn't you? ● . . . | *Am I right?* | 1 | 2 ✓ |
| | *Agree with me* | 1 | 2 |

EXERCISE

	1	2	3	4	5	6
Am I right?		✓		✓		
Agree with me	✓		✓	✓		

FOR THE TEACHER: FURTHER WORK
(Many students have difficulty producing the falling tone, because of their tendency to use a rising tone for questions.)

1 You can ask students to imitate both kinds of question tag, spoken by a native speaker.

2 You may show pictures of people, scenes, etc. which students will be able to both recognise and describe easily.

    T What's this?/What's she doing?/etc.
    S It's a . . ., isn't it./She's . . . ing, isn't she./etc.

If a student uses a rising tone, say:

    T Can't you see properly?/Aren't you sure?/etc.

This will show students when they have expressed uncertainty in their intonation.

1·3
Which car did it? (*page* 5)

TAPESCRIPT OF EXERCISE

Examples. First, just listen to the people from Tappa Typewriters talking. Did the red car hit the blue car? Or did the blue car hit the red car?

Policeman: Now you saw the accident. Tell me what happened.
Woman: The red car ran into the blue one. That's what happened. ●
Response: So the red one did it.
Guide voice: So the red one did it.
Policeman: I see. What did you see, sir?
Man: As far as I could see, the red car was run into by the blue one. ●
Response: So the blue one did it.
Guide voice: So the blue one did it.

Now do the exercise. After each BLEEP, say which car apparently caused the accident.

Policeman: Right. Now then, Mr Smith. What did you see?
Mike Smith: Well, it's quite simple really. The red car crashed into the blue one. ●
Response: _____
Guide voice: So the red one did it.
Policeman: I see. Mr er Peter Crane? What about you?
Peter Crane: Well now, as far as I could see, the blue car was travelling fast out of town and I guess it was hit by the red car. ●
Response: _____
Guide voice: So the red one did it.
Policeman: Right. Miss Daly? Could I hear what you saw?
Christine: Yes, of course, Officer. I saw the red car going towards town and then suddenly it was hit by the blue one. ●
Response: _____
Guide voice: So the blue one did it.
Policeman: Thank you. Now, who else saw the crash? Oh, you did, young man. Right, well, what happened, then?
Young man: Well, I could see this blue car coming past the swimming pool, and then the red car comes along and smashes into him. ●
Response: _____
Guide voice: So the red one did it.
Policeman: I see. You want to say something, Miss?
Secretary: Yes, I saw the accident from the window just here. And the blue car came along and the red one was just smashed into pieces. ●
Response: _____
Guide voice: So the blue one did it.
Policeman: Right. Thank you, Miss. Anyone else? Oh? Yes, sir?

Old man: I saw it too. I saw the red car. It was going much too fast and the blue car . . . it was going right, you see . . . and the red one crashed straight into it. ●
Response: _____
Guide voice: So the red one did it.

NOTE

The young man (Item 4) uses the Present Simple to describe a past event ('And then the red car **comes** along . . .'). This is quite common in colloquial English.

1·4
Who is the doer? Mike himself or someone else?
(*page* 6)

NOTE

1 When used in this sense, 'had' is never shortened to ''d'. E.g. I had my car mended. (NOT: I'd my car mended.)

2 In informal language, 'get' can be used in the same way as 'have', to mean 'arrange for someone else to do it'. E.g. I'm getting the car mended. = I'm arranging for the car to be mended. (by someone else)

3 'Have something done' can also mean 'experience something'. E.g. I had my bike stolen last week.

TAPESCRIPT OF EXERCISE

Examples. First, just listen to Mike. Is he talking about doing the things himself or about arranging for someone else to do them?

Mike: Just a minute, Mr Brown . . . Yes . . . I've just checked the order book and . . . ●
Response: Mike himself.
Guide voice: Mike himself.
Mike: Yes, of course. Don't worry, I'll have them sent to your new address. ●
Response: Someone else.
Guide voice: Someone else.

Now do the exercise. After each BLEEP, say 'Mike himself', or 'Someone else'.

Mike: Yes, I'm afraid I sent my last letter to your old address. ●
Response: _____
Guide voice: Mike himself.
Mike: Well, of course. I'll have the other goods sent off to you at once. ●
Response: _____
Guide voice: Someone else.
Mike: But I had your account checked only last week, Mr Brown. ●
Response: _____
Guide voice: Someone else.
Mike: Yes, Mr Brown. I've checked your machine carefully and there's really nothing wrong with it. ●
Response: _____
Guide voice: Mike himself.
Mike: Of course, Mr Brown. I'll have your receipt sent off, as soon as we get your cheque. ●
Response: _____
Guide voice: Someone else.
Mike: No, I'm afraid I'm not in on Monday. I'm having the office painted. Monday won't be convenient. ●
Response: _____
Guide voice: Someone else.
Mike: Tuesday will be fine. Goodbye, Mr Brown.

1·5
Is he asking a question?
(*page* 7)

PRACTICE POINT

Interrupting and finishing off someone else's sentence is something people do in most languages. If we do not recognise that this is happening, and if we think that the person interrupting us is asking a '*Wh*' question, we may answer it and confusion will arise.

NOTE

'*Wh*' clauses can also come at the beginning of a sentence in conversational English. However, this is less common than at the end. E.g. Where he is, I can't imagine. How he did that is a mystery.

TAPESCRIPT OF EXERCISE

Examples. First, just listen to Mike and Christine. When Mike interrupts Christine, is he asking her a new question, or is he finishing her sentence for her?

Christine: Oh . . . sorry to bother you, Mike. I'm afraid I haven't a clue –
Mike: What the time is. ● . . .
Christine: Right. Anyway, now I'm here. I'm not sure –
Mike: Why didn't you come and see me before?
● . . .

Now do the exercise. After each BLEEP, write your answer in the Workbook.

Christine: Well . . . it's a bit difficult, in fact. You see, I don't really know –
Mike: What's the problem? ● . . .
Christine: It's all these new machines. I just can't see –
Mike: How we're going to get rid of them. ● . . .
Christine: That's right. I mean, I don't know –
Mike: How many are there exactly? ● . . .
Christine: About 50,000 . . . but I'm not quite sure –
Mike: Where are they all at the moment? ● . . .
Christine: In the warehouse . . . And that's the other thing, I don't know –
Mike: How long we can leave them there. ● . . .
Christine: Yes, I'm not sure –
Mike: How much is it costing us per week? ● . . .
Christine: That's what's worrying me.

KEY

Example

1 ⊙

2 ⑦

Exercise

1 ⑦

2 ⊙

3 ⑦

4 ⑦

5 ⊙

6 ⑦

1·6
Please could you tell me . . . ?
(NATURAL SPEECH) (*page* 8)

QUESTIONS

A: this is to practise general understanding. It does not matter at this stage if individual words and phrases are not fully understood.

TAPESCRIPT OF EXERCISE

A *Secretary:* Right. There's the 9.09 . . .
Donald: Mm.
Secretary: . . . which gets in at 9.42
Donald: Mm.
Secretary: The 9.17 which . . .
Donald: No.
Secretary: . . . ge . . .
Donald: Yes.
Secretary: . . . gets in at 10 o'clock.

Donald: Yes, there aren't any fast ones, are there.
Secretary: Well, the 9 . . . 9.09 that gets in at 9.42, that would be[1] a fast one.
Donald: Mm. There's nothing quicker than that is there.
Secretary: No. No, that's about the fastest. . . .
Donald: How about[2] fast ones later in the morning?
Secretary: Ermmm. There's a 10.07.
Donald: Yeh. That takes about half an hour to get in, doesn't it.
{*Secretary:* Yeah, 10.07 gets in at 10.40, so that's . . . what . . . 31 minutes?
{*Donald:* Yeah.
{*Secretary:* Something like that.
{*Donald:* Yeah.
Secretary: Yeah.
Donald: Um. Could you just repeat that again? I'll take that data. The first one was . . .
Secretary: There's the 9.09
Donald: 9.09 getting in at . . .
Secretary: Or there's another one here which is the 9.41 . . .
Donald: 9.49 . . . 41
Secretary: that gets in at 10.14
Donald: 10.14. Yeah, that's a fast one, isn't . . .
Secretary: And then the 10.07 . . .

B *Secretary:* Hallo. Judith Marshall.
Tom: Hallo, Judith. This is Tom here.
Secretary: Yes.
Tom: Um . . . d'you think you could look up a . . . train time for me, please?
Secretary: Yes, certainly. Hold on.

Tom: I'm er having my car serviced, so I've got to go home to train . . . *by* train today.
Secretary: Right, OK, hold on.
Tom: Thank you.
Secretary: D'you want to go from here?
Tom: Yes, um . . . I want to go to . . . Great Chesterford.
Secretary: Right. . . . There's . . . one . . . at . . . quarter past four . . .
Tom: I see. Er . . . that one doesn't stop at Audley End, does it.
Secretary: Er, yes, it does.
Tom: Ah . . . Is there one that *doesn't* stop at Audley End? A bit later perhaps?
Secretary: Yes. . . . 4.35.
{*Tom:* OK, right, that's fine. . . .
{*Secretary:* OK?
{*Tom:* Thank you very much. Bye.[3]
{*Secretary:* Right. Cheerio.[4]

NOTES

1 would be = is (tentative/polite)
2 how about = tell me about (informal)
3 bye = goodbye (informal)
4 cheerio = goodbye (informal)

NOTE ALSO

1 Asking someone to do something:
D'you think you could . . . (polite)
Could you . . . (polite)
2 Identifying on the telephone:
Judith: Hallo. Judith Marshall.
Tom: Hallo, Judith. This is Tom here.

KEY

A 1  2

B 1 Barlow	9.09	9.17	9.41	10.07
London	9.42	10.00	10.14	10.40

2 He's asking a question. 3 He's expecting her to agree. 4 He's expecting her to agree. 5a) data 5b) I'll write down that information.

C 1a) hold on 1b) wait; or hang on; or just a minute; *etc.* 2a) serviced 2b) Someone else is repairing the car. 3 He's asking a question.

2·1
Opinion or doubt? (*page* 11)

PRACTICE POINT

1 'I think' is very frequently used in spoken English to express either opinion or doubt.

2 When 'think' is used in these senses it is never used in a progressive form. E.g. I think he's happy. (NOT: I'm thinking he's happy.)

NOTE

1 *Negative*

An opinion	Uncertainty
I don't think he's coming.	I don't think he's coming.

2 *Asking for an opinion*

What d'you think about it?
D'you think he's coming?

TAPESCRIPT OF EXERCISE

Examples. First, just listen to Peter and Christine. When do they mean, 'This is an opinion'? When do they mean 'This is uncertain'?

Christine: I think we'd better start ... ● ...
  Have you heard from Harry?
Peter: Oh ... he's really working hard at the moment

  ... but he *thinks* the sales model'll be ready on time. ● ...

Now do the exercise. After each BLEEP, tick the appropriate box in the Workbook.

Christine: Good. Well then ... we can start planning,

  I suppose. I *think* we're expected to visit all the major cities on that list there. ● ...
Peter: That'll be quite a job, won't it. Mind you, it'll

  be worth it. Mike thinks this model's going to be a fantastic success. ● ...
Christine: Mmm. I'm sure he's right. In fact, I was

  reading a market report this morning and I *think* they said the market had never been so good. ● ...

But I think we're still going to have to set up a pretty big advertising campaign. ● ...
Christine: So we'd better start. Oh, just a minute,

I *think* I just heard John come in. ● ...
There was a message from him on my desk and

I *think* he wants to have a word with me. ● ...
Peter: OK. Well, I'll wait around here till you get back. Don't be long.

KEY

FOR THE TEACHER: FURTHER WORK

1 Ask for the students' opinions to elicit 'I think'.

2 Show the students a very unusual picture. Ask 'What's this?'

3 Listen to recorded discussions. Ask your students to interpret the meaning of 'I think', 'I imagine', 'I suppose', *etc.*

2·2
Did they see it themselves or not? (*page* 13)

PRACTICE POINT

The word 'apparently' is used frequently. It indicates that the speaker is offering someone else's opinion and not his own.

DOING THE EXERCISE

In the sentence: 'The car seemed to just jump in the air', 'just' means 'simply'.

TAPESCRIPT OF EXERCISE

Examples. First, just listen to the group of friends talking. Which of them saw the accident? Which of them didn't?

Man: There was an accident at the race this afternoon, apparently. ● . . .
Woman: Yes, I know . . . a terrible one. The whole place seemed suddenly to go mad. ● . . .

Now do the exercise. After each BLEEP, write 'Yes' or 'No' in the Workbook.

Maggie: Awful! The car seemed to just jump in the air. ● . . .
Joanna: It was going terribly fast at the time, apparently. ● . . .
Christine: Yes, but the driver appeared to be quite unhurt. ● . . .
Mike: Lucky man, if you ask me. It seems he was able to simply walk away from the wreckage. ● . . .
Peter: Well, yes . . . but as soon as he reached the edge of the track he collapsed, apparently. ● . . .
American girl: But the awful thing was that another car crashed into the wreckage . . . it seemed to just swerve and then it just burst into flames. ● . . .

KEY

Examples
1 No
2 Yes

Exercise
1 Yes
2 No
3 Yes
4 No
5 No
6 Yes

2·3
Is it logical or is it nonsense?
(*page* 15)

PRACTICE POINT

1 'Therefore', 'and so', and 'must' are words (or signals) which show the relationship between two facts.

2 The second statement of each pair contains one of these signals, and therefore it appears as the result of the first statement.

3 'Therefore' is used especially in formal English (spoken or written).

DOING THE EXERCISE

Students should:
1 Listen for the signals ('therefore', 'and so', 'must').
2 Decide whether the second fact is the *logical* result of the first.

TAPESCRIPT OF EXERCISE

Examples. First, just listen to Joanna reading parts of the translated scripts. Is what she reads logical or illogical?

Joanna: The last harvest was very bad and so there is now plenty of food. ● . . .
Joanna: The last harvest was very bad. The people must be very short of food. ● . . .

Now do the exercise. After each BLEEP, tick the appropriate box in the Workbook.

Joanna: In 1959, the USSR had a very good harvest and was, therefore, forced to buy food from the United States of America. ● . . .
Joanna: This year's harvest is even worse than last year's. We shall, therefore, have to increase our food imports. ● . . .
Joanna: In spite of the bad harvest, the Government refused to import extra food. The people must've been very hungry that year. ● . . .
Joanna: There is a terrible shortage of food in the country. The people have been ordered, therefore, to eat more. ● . . .

KEY

EXAMPLES

1 *Joanna:* The last harvest was very bad and so there is now plenty of food. ● . . .

Logical | 1 | 2
Illogical | 1 ✓ | 2

2 *Joanna:* The last harvest was very bad. The people must now be short of food. ● . . .

Logical | 1 | 2 ✓
Illogical | 1 | 2

EXERCISE

Logical | 1 | 2 ✓ | 3 ✓ | 4
Illogical | 1 ✓ | 2 | 3 | 4 ✓

FOR THE TEACHER: FURTHER WORK
Oral or written:
Provide students with a statement.
Get the students to supply a logical statement of result with 'therefore', 'and so', 'must', *etc.*
E.g. *T* He hardly slept at all last night.
     S He must be very tired.
  or *S* And so he's very tired.

2·4

Is someone unable to do it now? Or is it impossible that someone did it in the past? (*page* 17)

PRACTICE POINT

1 'Can't have' is contracted in spoken English to 'can't've'.

2 'Can't have done' expresses a logical negative deduction about a past event.

    E.g. *A* He didn't even say 'Hello'.
            B He can't have recognised you.

3 'Must have done' expresses a logical affirmative deduction about a past event.

    E.g. *A* He felt really ill after that party.
            B He must have eaten too much.

These forms are fully dealt with in general course books.

DOING THE EXERCISE

Example 2: 'they can't've . . .' 'They' here is used in a general sense to mean the person who had the book before.

TAPESCRIPT OF EXERCISE

Examples. First, just listen to Mike and Christine. Does Christine mean 'Unable now' or 'Apparently impossible in the past'?

Mike: Where's Peter?
Christine: Oh, he can't make it after all. ● . . .
Mike: OK. Well, never mind. Now where's the order book?
Christine: Oh dear, I'm afraid they can't've sent it up. But don't worry . . . I'll go and get it. ● . . .

Now do the exercise. After each BLEEP, tick the appropriate box in the Workbook.

Mike: Good, well now . . . what about the new Swiss customer? Any news from him?
Christine: Oh, him. He can't send us an order this month. ● . . .
Mike: Oh . . . I see . . . and what about the German order?
Christine: Well, he can't've sent one . . . Mm. That's a bit worrying. ● . . .
Mike: Well, we'll wait and see what happens there. How's the Smith account?
Christine: Um, yes, I checked that and he can't've paid it, whatever he says . . . ● . . .
Mike: But what about the money he owes us then?
Christine: Huh . . . I bet he can't pay us even half of it. ● . . .
Mike: Aah. Oh well. Oh, by the way, I've been getting enquiries about that big order for Italy.
Christine: Oh, yes . . . I've been looking into it . . . and er . . . you know, they can't've sent it. ● . . .

Mike: Well, do what you can about it, will you? And one more question, Christine, before you go, what's happening about the Spanish order?
Christine: Oh that. Yes. Well, I'm afraid we can't meet it. ● . . .

KEY

EXAMPLES

1 *Mike:* Where's Peter?
Christine: Oh, he can't make it after all. ● . . .

Unable (now) — 1 ✓   2
Impossible (past) — 1   2

2 *Mike:* OK. Well, never mind. Now where's the order book?
Christine: Oh dear, I'm afraid they can't've sent it up. But don't worry. I'll go and get it. ● . . .

Unable (now) — 1   2
Impossible (past) — 1   2 ✓

EXERCISE

	1	2	3	4	5	6
Unable (now)	✓		✓		✓	
Impossible (past)		✓	✓		✓	

2·5
What does it mean? (*page* 19)

PRACTICE POINT

Guessing the meaning of unknown words or phrases is a very important skill. It is a good idea to practise it as often as possible.

DOING THE EXERCISE

The exact wording of the answers does not matter, provided they have the same general meaning as the answers in the key.

TAPESCRIPT OF EXERCISE

First, just listen to Maggie and Graham.

Maggie: Oh, hello. I'm so sorry I'm late, Graham. I knew we'd arranged to meet at one-thirty, but the place completely slipped my mind. In the end, I had to phone your secretary, and, fortunately, she had it in her diary or something and so she told me to come here.

Graham: Oh . . . don't worry. I was a bit late too. That new office boy really has got a memory like a sieve. I had to ask him four times to bring me the order book this morning and he finally brought it just as I was about to leave.

Maggie: Oh dear . . . well, never mind. Let's look at the menu . . . Oh, by the way, you remember you were asking me about that place in Greece . . . (*Graham:* Mmm?)
And I said I didn't know it . . . ? Well, it suddenly came to me in a flash while I was in the bath last night . . . it's called *Spoulos*.

Graham: Oh yes, of course. That's it. In fact someone did tell me the name, but it just went in one ear and out of the other as usual! That's why I thought of asking you if you knew. Spoulos. Mm. I'll try to remember it this time.

Now listen to Maggie again. What do you think 'It slipped my mind' means? After the BLEEP, write your answer in the Workbook.

Maggie: Oh, hello. I'm so sorry I'm late, Graham. I knew we'd arranged to meet at one-thirty, but the place completely slipped my mind. In the end, I had to phone your secretary, and, fortunately, she had it in her diary or something and so she told me to come here. ● . . .

Now listen to Graham again. What do you think 'He's got a memory like a sieve' means? After the BLEEP, write your answer in the Workbook.

Graham: Oh . . . don't worry. I was a bit late too. That new office boy really has got a memory like a sieve. I had to ask him four times to bring me the order book this morning and he finally brought it just as I was about to leave. ● . . .

Now listen to Maggie again. What do you think 'It came to me in a flash' means? After the BLEEP, write your answer in the Workbook.

Maggie: Oh dear . . . well, never mind. Let's look at the menu . . . Oh, by the way, you remember you were asking me about that place in Greece . . . (*Graham:* Mmm?) And I said I didn't know it . . . ? Well, it suddenly came to me in a flash while I was in the bath last night . . . it's called *Spoulos*. ● . . .

Now listen to Graham again. What do you think 'It went in one ear and out the other' means? After the BLEEP, write your answer in the Workbook.

Graham: Oh yes, of course. That's it. In fact someone did tell me the name, but it just went in one ear and out the other, as usual! That's why I thought of asking you if you knew. Spoulos. Mm. I'll try to remember it this time. ● . . .

KEY

Example
Forget about the past.

Exercise
1 I forgot it.
2 He doesn't remember anything.
3 I suddenly remembered it.
4 I heard it but I didn't remember it.

> ### FOR THE TEACHER: FURTHER WORK
> 1 Select passages for listening or reading comprehension which contain words unknown to your students. Encourage the students to deduce their meaning.
> 2 Select passages for reading or listening comprehension and replace a few of the verbs, nouns, adjectives and adverbs with a nonsense word. Encourage the students to guess what sort of word the nonsense word has replaced.

2·6
Who does he think they are?
(NATURAL SPEECH) (*page* 20)

YOUR AIMS

When listening in order to answer Questions B to D, it will be helpful to look at the pictures that John is talking about.

QUESTIONS

A: this is to practise general understanding. It does not matter, at this stage, if individual words and phrases are not fully understood.

B4: there are more than four possible reasons why John thinks this man is 'Baby-Face Nelson'. Only *four* need to be mentioned in the answer.

D1*b*): the missing phrase has something to do with 'remembering/forgetting.'

TAPESCRIPT OF EXERCISE

Caroline: I showed John one of the pictures and asked him 'Who do you think this is?'

John: I – I think this fellow is um is a gangster from the thirties (Mm) erm . . . very sure of himself . . . t . . . mm bit flashy erm . . . probably someone very very famous . . . (mm) one could almost say he's baby-faced (mm) or is it someone called or is it Baby-Faced or . . . s . . . Baby-faced Nelson? I think it is (hmm) I'm sure it is (mhm) by the cut of his clothes 'nd 't looks like a cigar here (Mm) and . . . m I think for[1] what d'you say Mafia-looking only Italian[2] . . . very Italian-looking. I think so, any rate.[3]

Caroline: I then showed John another picture and asked him who he thought *this* was.

John: Well, I *still* say this is um this is er President Roosevelt . . . erm can't remember[4] when he was in power but I'm sure of it . . . I'm sure this is who

• •

it is. As my wife says I think he's writing music but um I thought he collected um stamps for a hobby . . . (President Roosevelt?) Mmm (mm) erm . . . can't really r see the details of what he's supposed to be doing. I think he's writing something. Looks very official-looking any rate.[3] And erm . . . quite old[5] as well.

Caroline: Then I showed John the third picture and said: 'Mmm. OK. What about him?'

John: Well, he puts me in the mind[6] of what my forefathers were supposed to look like . . . (*laugh*) very upright, very miserable-looking erm shouldn't think[7] he's ever cracked his face to laugh[8] I shouldn't think. Um (Mm?) . . . Wouldn't like him for a next-door neighbour any rate.[3] (*Laugh.* Why not?) Well, he looks really miserable. Looks as if you'd shut the door[9] a bit noisy[10] he'd be be knocking at the door . . . God, he's miserable isn't he. (Yeh)

NOTES

1 I think for = I think (slip of the tongue)
2 Mafia-looking only Italian = Mafia -looking . . . Italian (slip of the tongue)
3 any rate = at any rate (informal)
4 can't remember = I can't remember (informal)
5 quite old = he's quite old (informal)
6 in the mind of = in mind of (slip of the tongue)
7 shouldn't think = I shouldn't think (informal)
8 he's ever cracked his face to laugh = he's ever relaxed enough to laugh.
9 looks as if you'd shut = looks as if, if you'd shut . . . (slip of the tongue)
10 noisy = noisily (non-standard)

NOTE ALSO

Typical features of John's London accent

	standard English		London accent
1	fellow	pronounced	fella
2	it is		i'is
	cut of		cu'of
	but I'm		bu'I'm
	quite old		qui'old
3	looking		lookin'
	writing		writin'
4	still		stiu
5	isn't he		inti

KEY

A

2nd

1st

3rd

B1*a*) thirties 1*b*) He was a gangster between 1930 and 1940. 2 opinion 3*a*) cut 3*b*) style 4 Any *four* of these reasons: Because he's baby-faced. Because of the style of his clothes. Because he looks Italian. Because he looks like a member of the Mafia. Because he's holding a cigar. Because he looks flashy. Because he looks self-confident.

C1 no 2 yes; his wife 3 opinion

D1*a*) puts me in the mind 1*b*) reminds me 2 unpleasant 3 He would be unfriendly.

3·1
What was that word?
(page 23)

PRACTICE POINT

1 The 'echo question' is not normally dealt with in
general course books. However, it is fairly common.

2 Without the introductory phrase 'I'm sorry', the
echo question can sound impolite or, at least,
very informal.

NOTE

Echo questions of this kind can be used with 'where',
'who/whom', 'when', and 'what', but *not* usually
with 'why' or 'how'.

TAPESCRIPT OF EXERCISE

Example. First, just listen to Maggie.

Maggie: I'd like a ATCHOO ●
Response: I'm sorry? You'd like a what?
Guide voice: I'm sorry? You'd like a what?

Now go on. After each BLEEP, ask Maggie your echo
questions.

Maggie: Oh never mind. D'you think you could pass
my bag? I'd like a ATCHOO . . . ●
Response: _____
Guide voice: I'm sorry? You'd like a what?
Maggie: An aspirin. Oh gosh . . . this cold. (*sniff*)
Mind you, what I'd like *more* is a glass of
ATCHOOO . . . ●
Response: _____
Guide voice: I'm sorry? You'd like a glass of what?
Maggie: Whisky . . . No, perhaps it's not a very good
idea. But I'd love a ATCHOOO . . . ●
Response: _____
Guide voice: I'm sorry? You'd love a what?

Maggie: (*groan/sniff*) Oh dear . . . a cup of tea, if you
can manage. Oh . . . I'm so sorry to be like this
now you're here. I've been longing to ATCHOOO . . .
● . . .
Response: _____
Guide voice: I'm sorry? You've been longing to what?
Maggie: To see you, of course. I must say, I *hate*
having a ATCHOOO . . . ●
Response: _____
Guide voice: I'm sorry? You hate having a what?
Maggie: Ugh . . . A cold. In fact I think I'd rather
ATCHOOO . . . ●
Response: _____
Guide voice: I'm sorry? You'd rather what . . . ?
Maggie: I'd rather die . . . ATCHOOOOOOOOOOOO . . .

3·2
Tell me about her,
or tell me what she likes
(*page* 24)

PRACTICE POINT

1 In spoken English, these two questions sound very similar.

> What does she like?
> What is she like?

2 In other tenses the similarity is not so great.

> E.g. What'll she like?
> What'll she be like?

DOING THE EXERCISE

1 In Items 1 and 6: 'What's she like *then*?' and 'See you later *then*', the word 'then' is not a 'time' adverb. It means 'so' or 'therefore' ('So what's she like?', 'So I'll see you later'). 'Then' is frequently used in this way in informal speech.
2 'See you later' is frequently used in informal speech to mean 'goodbye', if we expect to see the other person in the (near) future.

TAPESCRIPT OF EXERCISE

Examples. First, just listen to Peter. Does he want to know about the woman herself? Or does he want to know what she likes?

Peter: Hello . . . Just waiting for the typist. She's coming back today. I wonder what she'll be like after her illness. ● . . .

Peter: I don't know. What do *you* think she'd like? ● . . .

Now do the exercise. After each BLEEP, tick the appropriate box in the Workbook.

Peter: Yes . . . OK . . . I hear you've got a new assistant. What's she like then? ● . . .

Peter: Yes . . . That's a good idea . . . What does she like, d'you know? ● . . .

Peter: No, our new Swiss customer . . . We're meeting her for lunch. I wonder what she'll like after her journey. ● . . .

Peter: (*laughs*) Oh, *her*! Yes, she's bad enough in a crowd. What would she be like alone . . . ● . . .

Peter: Oh, what d'*you* think she's like then? ● . . .

Peter: No . . . I'm just wondering what she'd like, that's all. ● . . .

Peter: OK. See you later then. Bye for now.

KEY

EXAMPLES

1 *Peter:* Hello. Just waiting for the typist. She's coming back today. I wonder what she'll be like after her illness. ● . . .			
She herself	✓		
What she likes			

2 *Peter:* I don't know. What do *you* think she'd like? ● . . .			
She herself			
What she likes		✓	

EXERCISE

	1	2	3	4	5	6
She herself	✓			✓	✓	
What she likes		✓	✓			✓

FOR THE TEACHER: FURTHER WORK

Try to use the questions practised here as much as possible in your classes.

3·3
Is she interested or not?
(*page* 26)

PRACTICE POINT

Oh ⤵ = enthusiasm
Oh ⤸ = lack of enthusiasm } These different pronunciations of 'oh' and other interjections are fairly common in European languages.

DOING THE EXERCISE

Example 1: 'I was wondering if . . .' is a polite way of beginning when we ask or invite someone to do something.
Item 4: 'the short film' and 'the main one'. In many British cinemas two films are shown during one programme.
Item 5: Racquel Welch is a famous American filmstar.
Item 6: Paul Newman is also a famous American filmstar.

TAPESCRIPT OF EXERCISE

Examples. First, just listen to Peter and Joanna. Is Joanna interested in what Peter tells her, or not?

Peter: Hello? Joanna? Oh, hello. I was wondering if you'd like to go out this evening.

⤵
Joanna: Oh ● . . .
Peter: I was thinking about a Jazz concert . . .

⤸
Joanna: Oh ● . . .

Now do the exercise. After each BLEEP, draw the appropriate mouth in the Workbook.

Peter: Then I remembered I'd got these two free tickets for the cinema.

⤵
Joanna: Oh ● . . .
Peter: Yeah. And we're in luck. There's a really good film on. It's an 'X' . . .

⤸
Joanna: Oh ● . . .
Peter: Don't worry. You'll love it. It's all about Chicago night-life.

⤵
Joanna: Oh ● . . .
Peter: Well, anyway . . . that's only the short film. The main one's a Western.

⤸
Joanna: Oh ● . . .
Peter: With Racquel Welch . . .

⤸
Joanna: Oh ● . . .
Peter: And Paul Newman.

⤵
Joanna: Oh ● . . .
Peter: Well, anyway. How about it. Are you coming or not?
Joanna: Thanks Peter. I'd love to. What time . . .

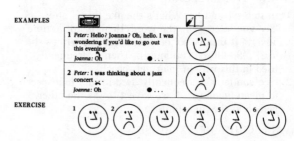

EXAMPLES

1 *Peter:* Hello? Joanna? Oh, hello. I was wondering if you'd like to go out this evening.
Joanna: Oh ● . . .

2 *Peter:* I was thinking about a jazz concert . . .
Joanna: Oh ● . . .

EXERCISE   1 2 3 4 5 6

3·4
Has he finished speaking?
(*page 27*)

PRACTICE POINT

1 When more than two items are being listed, the word 'and' is generally omitted before each item *except* the last.
E.g. I'd like an omelette, a salad and a lemonade.

2 When we are thinking at the same time as speaking, however, we sometimes insert the word 'and' between each item.

E.g. I'd like an omelette and a salad and a lemonade. A rising tone is normally used on all items except the last.

3 If a native speaker uses a *down* tone in the *middle* of a list, he will nearly always say 'erm' to indicate that the list is not complete.

DOING THE EXERCISE

'I guess' (in the filmstar's last comment: 'And Cat Stevens, I guess') is commonly used in American English. It means 'I suppose' or 'I think'.

TAPESCRIPT OF EXERCISE

Examples. First, just listen to the American filmstar. When he hesitates, is he going to add something more? Or has he finished all he wants to say?

American: W-e-ell, I just lo-o-ve rice and fish . . . ●
Response: Yes?
Guide voice: Yes?

American: Well, as I was saying, I just love rice 'nd

fish 'nd tomato sauce. ●
Response: I see.
Guide voice: I see.

Now do the exercise. After each BLEEP, say 'Yes?' or 'I see'.

American: And I suppose you want to know what drinks I like and so on . . . Well, I guess I don't

much care for whisky . . . ●
Response: _____
Guide voice: Yes?

American: And I don't care for rum . . . ●
Response: _____
Guide voice: Yes?

American: And I don't like lemonade at all. ●
Response: _____
Guide voice: I see.

American: And my favourite music is my own . . .
●
Response: _____
Guide voice: Yes?

American: And Cat Stevens, I guess. ●
Response: _____
Guide voice: I see.

3·5
Is this surprising or not?
(*page 28*)

PRACTICE POINT

1 Certain words and phrases show what is going to happen next in a conversation. Being able to recognise them is a great help in comprehension.

2 These introduce a 'surprising' fact:
    'however' (the most formal of the four used in this exercise)
    'although'
    'and yet'
    'but'
They are sometimes called 'concessive conjuncts'.

3 These add a similar and therefore a not surprising fact:
    'and'
    'also'
    'what is (what's) more'   These tend to be
    'moreover'   used in more
    'not only . . . but also'   formal English.

NOTE

'Not only' is followed by an inversion of the main verb.
E.g. He lied and he also stole.

   Not only did he lie { but he stole as well.
                    but he also stole.

TAPESCRIPT OF EXERCISE

Examples. First, just listen to Maggie and Graham.

Graham: Hello? Maggie? Oh, hello. What's the hotel like? Is it comfortable?

Maggie: Well, yes, on the whole, it's very comfortable but the food . . . (*crackle*) ● . . .

Graham: And what about the people? Nice?

Maggie: Oh, yes. The room-staff are really nice 'n' friendly, and what is more, the waiters . . . (*crackle*) ● . . .

Now do the exercise. After each BLEEP, tick the words which you think should end Maggie's sentence.

Graham: And the other guests?

Maggie: Oh, very pleasant. There are some children, however, who are . . . (*crackle*) ● . . .

Graham: What's the beach like? There *is* a beach, I suppose?

Maggie: Yes, and although it's a bit small and crowded, it's . . . (*crackle*) ● . . .

Graham: Well that's the main thing.

Maggie: Yes, that's true. The sand's swept every morning and moreover the sea . . . (*crackle*) ● . . .

Graham: Is it warm? The sea, I mean.

Maggie: No. It isn't as warm as I was hoping it would be and yet . . . (*crackle*) ● . . .

Graham: How was the plane, by the way?

Maggie: The plane? Oh, it was really annoying. Not only did we start late but . . . (*crackle*) ● . . .

Graham: Look, Maggie . . . this line's awful. I think we'd better stop. I hope things go well for you. See you next week. Bye!

Maggie: Bye-bye, Graham. Thanks for calling.

KEY

EXAMPLES

1 *Graham:* Hello? *Maggie:* What's the hotel like? Is it comfortable? *Maggie:* Well, yes, on the whole it's very comfortable but the food . . . (*crackle*) ● . . .	a) isn't good		b) is very good ✓	2 *Graham:* And what about the people? Nice? *Maggie:* Oh, yes. The room-staff are really nice and friendly and, what is more, the waiters . . . (*crackle*) ● . . .	a) are unhelpful		b) are excellent ✓

EXERCISE

1	a) very sweet		4	a) it's quite pleasant enough	✓
	b) rather noisy	✓		b) it's very unpleasant	
2	a) very clean	✓	5	a) we arrived on time	
	b) very dirty			b) we arrived late, too	✓
3	a) is clean	✓			
	b) is dirty, too				

FOR THE TEACHER: FURTHER WORK

Listen, with your students, to a discussion in English on tape. Stop the machine immediately you hear one of the above signals. Encourage your students to guess what sort of thing the speaker is going to say.

3·6
What do they like eating?
(NATURAL SPEECH) (*page* 30)

SITUATION

Bob Giddens (the fourth person interviewed) has a London accent.

QUESTIONS

A: this is to practise general understanding. It does not matter, at this stage, if individual words and phrases are not fully understood. The answers to Question A should be based on:
 i) tone/age of voice of the speaker
 ii) sex of speaker
 iii) the kind of food enjoyed, which may indicate the age of the speaker
 iv) other personal information given by the speaker

D1: One may assume that his mother is not *always* working, nor is Gareth always doing examinations.

TAPESCRIPT OF EXERCISE

Interviewer: Now, are you . . . very interested in eating and food?

Susan Johns: . . . I have a very dodgy stomach which rather . . . prevents me getting too carried away with it. I . . . I do . . . I mean I love going out to eat but that's the whole atmosphere of eating out rather than . . . eating in.

Interviewer: What sort of things do you normally eat for . . . supper?

Tony Blakemore: Oh . . . we eat a great variety of things . . . er fish, . . . meat . . . though . . . that tends to be[1] sort of[2] cheaper-f-cuts of meat rather than . . . things like steak and joints.

Interviewer: What sort of things do you usually eat for supper?

Gareth Jones: . . . Well, when I was doing my exams 'n' my mother's working it tends[3] to be . . . convenience foods-s . . . frozen foods just to save time really, such as steak'n'kidney pies, 'n'fish-fingers, 'n'sausages.

Interviewer: What sort of dishes do you like?

Bob Giddens: I like goin' out to a restaurant, 'n' havin' a nice [really][4] cooked meal, you know, like the steak;[5] but my favourite dish is roast pork and er with lashings of erm apple sauce, you know.[6] I think that's what makes roast pork for me, you know.[6]

Interviewer: If I asked you to just give me a list of about five things that you like eating most, could you do that?

Bob Giddens: (sighs) Eating most . . . oh . . . it's hard to say, you know, it . . . it . . . varies, you know. If[7] one day you could fancy something, you know, as your favourite and another day you know you've gone completely off of it.[8] I suppose um corned beef . . . ooph . . . various things you know, it's . . . I don't really know.

Interviewer: What sort of dishes do you like?

Mike Smith: Erm . . . I quite like spaghetti erm ice cream, chocolates, fruit . . . I like a lot of fruit . . . erm and salads erm . . . 'm also quite partial to beans – (laughs) baked beans.

NOTES

1 tends to be = is usually
2 sort of = kind of (used here as an informal 'filler', used when the speaker is not sure what word to use)
3 I was doing . . . it tends – Gareth mixes his tenses here
4 [really] – this word is not very clear.
5 the steak = steak (slip of the tongue)
6 you know – Bob Giddens uses this phrase frequently. He uses it to add force to what he is saying, but it is also a sign of lack of confidence. (informal)
7 If one day = one day (slip of the tongue)
8 off of it = off it (non-standard)

NOTE ALSO

Typical features of Bob's London accent

	standard English		London accent
1	meal	pronounced	miu
2	lashings		lashin's
3	having		'avin'
4	steak		stike
	day		die

KEY

A

A record producer Tony Blakemore

A student Gareth Jones

A building maintenance man Bob Giddens

A schoolboy Mike Smith

An executive Susan Johns

B1a) dodgy 1b) weak 2a) a meal at a restaurant 2b) a meal at home 2c) the atmosphere of 'eating out'

C1 cheaper cuts of meat 2 no

D1 no 2 yes

E1a) lashings 1b) a lot of 2a) makes 2b) roast pork and apple sauce together is best 2c) opinion 3a) fancy 3b) want 3c) people in general 4 You no longer like it.

F1a) partial 1b) yes

4·1
Is Mike unsure,
or is he annoyed?
(*page* 33)

PRACTICE POINT

1 This structure 'might have done', with its two meanings, is usually dealt with in general course books.

2 'Might have' is shortened in spoken English to 'might 've'.

3 The 'unsure' version can have various intonations, but if the 'uncertainty' is being *stressed*, the most usual intonation is the one shown in the Workbook.

4 Only one intonation is used to show annoyance. This is shown in the Workbook.

5 Voice-quality is also an important guide in distinguishing between these two meanings.

6 The 'annoyed' version is generally used only in spoken English or in an informal style of written English.

TAPESCRIPT OF EXERCISE

Examples. First, just listen to Mike. When is he unsure? When is he indignant?

Christine: Is Peter coming?

Mike: He said he was, but he might've been called away. ● . . .

Christine: Oh, yes . . . that's right. He's got an important customer to see this afternoon.

Mike: He might've mentioned it to me! ● . . .

Now do the exercise. After each BLEEP, tick the appropriate box in the Workbook.

Christine: Well, he only got the call after lunch. Anyway . . . let's get started. The first thing is that Barrington wrote last week.

Mike: What! You might've told me before! ● . . .

Christine: Yes, well . . . Anyway, he said he'd already sent an order.

Mike: Aha? Mmm. He might've sent one a month or so ago. ● . . .

Christine: Oh, and by the way . . . David says he only got five new customers while he was in France.

Mike: So I heard. He might've tried a bit harder! ● . . .

Christine: Hmm. He phoned the New York Office yesterday.

Mike: Honestly . . . he might've spoken to me first! ● . . .

Christine: Oh, well . . . anyway, we've got a meeting with the New York people next week, apparently.

Mike: Well, they might've given us a bit more time! ● . . .

Christine: So I'll go and ask Sue to book our flight, if she hasn't gone home.

Mike: She might've stayed late tonight. ● . . .

KEY

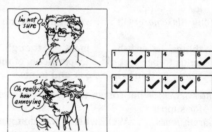

4·2
How do you say
you're sorry? (*page* 35)

PRACTICE POINT

'So sorry, awfully sorry, very sorry': these can all be casual *or* intense. They are *casual* when the subject and verbs are omitted, and when there is no stress on the adverbs 'so', 'awfully' and 'very'.

NOTE

'Sorry?' (with an upward intonation) is used in informal English to mean 'Please repeat what you said because I didn't hear properly'.

TAPESCRIPT OF EXERCISE

Examples. First, just listen to Peter apologising. Is he apologising for something serious? Or is he apologising for something unimportant?

Peter: Sorry about the lamp. ●
Response: Something unimportant.
Guide voice: Something unimportant.
Peter: I'm *so* sorry about the carpet. I can't think how I managed to do it. ●
Response: Something serious.
Guide voice: Something serious.

Now do the exercise. After each BLEEP, say 'Something serious', or 'Something unimportant'.

    (*Ouch!*)
Peter: Oh. I'm terribly sorry. I didn't realise there was anyone behind me. ●
Response: _____
Guide voice: Something serious.
    (*Ooh! Mind out!*)
Peter: Oops . . . sorry. Didn't see you. ●
Response: _____
Guide voice: Something unimportant.
    (*slight tinkle of glass*)
Peter: I'm sorry about the glass. ●
Response: _____
Guide voice: Something unimportant.
    (*different slight tinkle*)
Peter: I'm extremely sorry. I really don't know what to say. ●
Response: _____
Guide voice: Something serious.
Peter: I'm sorry to leave so early. I hope you don't mind. ●
Response: _____
Guide voice: Something unimportant.
    (*sound of protesting cat*)
Peter: I'm *so* sorry. I *do* hope it's all right. ●
Response: _____
Guide voice: Something serious.

FOR THE TEACHER: FURTHER WORK

Many learners of English misuse the words and phrases 'Excuse me', 'pardon', 'sorry' and 'I beg your pardon'. If your students are not clear about the differences, this would be a good time to talk about them.

4·3
Did it happen or not?
(*page* 36)

PRACTICE POINT

1 Recognising these two different intonation patterns is important. If we misunderstand what is meant, we may answer incorrectly and this could annoy the person we are speaking to.

> E.g.   A I thought you'd get here on time.
>
>   (= you *are* on time, as I expected)
>
> _____
>
>   B Yes, John gave me a lift. (Correct answer)
> *or*   B What do you mean? It's only 11.30!
>   I'm fifteen minutes early! (Incorrect answer because of misunderstanding)

2 Various different times can be meant:

> E.g.
> I thought it was going to rain.
>   = (and it DID rain/but it DIDN'T rain)
>   *or* (and it IS raining/but it ISN'T raining)
>
> _____
>
> I thought it would rain.
>   = (and it DID rain/but it DIDN'T rain)
>   *or* (and it IS raining/but it ISN'T raining)
>   *or* (and it HAS rained/but it HASN'T rained)
>
> _____
>
> I thought it would be raining.
>   = (and it IS raining/but it ISN'T raining)
>   *or* (and it WAS raining/but it WASN'T raining)
>
> _____
>
> I thought she would like it.
>   = (and she DOES like it/but she DOESN'T like it)
>   *or* (and she DID like it/ but she DIDN'T like it)
>
> _____
>
> I thought she'd (had) gone.
>   = (and she HAD gone/but she HADN'T gone)

DOING THE EXERCISE

Item 3: 'I rather thought'.
'Rather' generally makes a verb *less* strong, but here it is used ironically.

TAPESCRIPT OF EXERCISE

Examples. First, just listen to Joanna. Did things happen as she expected? Or did they not happen?

Joanna: Hello, Peter . . . are you having a good time?

Joanna: I thought you'd be having a lovely time. ● . . .

Joanna: I thought it would probably rain. ● . . .

Now do the exercise. After each BLEEP, write 'Yes' or 'No' in the Workbook.

Joanna: At the party? Oh, it wasn't too bad, really.

Mind you, I thought they'd all turn up to a party like that. ● . . .

Joanna: Yes, she came. I thought she was going to get drunk or something. ● . . .

Joanna: Mmm . . . I rather thought she'd apologise. ● . . .

Joanna: Yes, I suppose so. Yes, I thought your brother was going to phone me yesterday. ● . . .

Joanna: Oh . . . I thought you'd probably made a mistake. ● . . .

Joanna: Well, never mind. I thought you were coming over this evening. ● . . .
Joanna: Oh, OK, Bye!

KEY

Example	*Exercise*
1 No	1 Yes
2 Yes	2 No
	3 No
	4 No
	5 Yes
	6 No

4·4
Wish or regret? (*page* 38)

PRACTICE POINT

This structure (I wish . . .) is usually fully dealt with in general course books. However, it is often difficult for learners to understand the structure correctly in spoken English, in particular if we do not notice whether there is a 'd' sound at the end of the main verb or not.

E.g. I wish they'd **pay** their bills
   (= wish)
   I wish they'd **paid** their bills
   (= regret)

TAPESCRIPT OF EXERCISE

Examples. First, just listen to these people talking in their sleep. Are they hoping about something in the future? Or are they sorry about something in the past?

Maggie: I wish you'd booked in earlier. ● . . .
Joanna: I wish you'd take me with you. ● . . .

Now do the exercise. After each BLEEP, draw arrows by the corresponding pictures in the Workbook.

Mike: I wish we'd designed a smaller typewriter.
   ● . . .
Christine: Oh . . . I wish they'd pay their bills a bit quicker. ● . . .
Joanna: I wish he'd given me an easy essay to write.
   ● . . .
Peter: I wish he'd ordered several thousand machines.
   ● . . .
Maggie: Oh, I wish they'd send me their new brochures. ● . . .
Peter: I wish she'd come out and have dinner with me. ● . . .

KEY

EXAMPLES

		Future	Past
1 *Maggie:* I wish you'd booked in earlier. ● . . .			←
2 *Joanna:* I wish you'd take me with you. ● . . .		→	

EXERCISE

		Future	Past
1	←		
2	→		
3	←		
4	←		
5	→		
6	→		

Not at all, or only in special cases? (*page* 40)

PRACTICE POINT

This use of 'anyone' (〰.) etc. is common in spoken English. It is important to be able to recognise it and to understand what it means.

NOTE

The word 'any' can be used in the same way.

E.g. We won't accept at any price. 〰. •   (we definitely *won't* accept)
We won't accept at any price. 〰 •   (we *may* accept *but only* if we are offered the *best* conditions)

1 *Joanna:* Who? Mary? She doesn't go out with *anyone*, you know. ● . . .

Not at all [1] [2]

Only if . . . [1 ✓] [2]

2 *Joanna:* No. She told me. She doesn't like anybody. ● . . .

Not at all [1] [2 ✓]

Only if . . . [1] [2]

EXERCISE

Not at all [1] [2 ✓] [3] [4 ✓] [5] [6 ✓]

Only if . . . [1 ✓] [2] [3 ✓] [4] [5 ✓] [6]

TAPESCRIPT OF EXERCISE

Examples. First, just listen to Joanna. When does she mean 'Not at all', and when does she mean 'Only if it's a special case'?

Joanna: Who? Mary? She doesn't go out with anyone, 〰 • you know. ● . . .

Joanna: No. Well, if you ask me, she doesn't like

〰 . . .
anybody. ● . . .

Now do the exercise. After each BLEEP, tick the appropriate box in the Workbook.

Joanna: Oh, a meal. Yes, that'd be nice. But where?

〰 ✓
I don't want to eat anywhere. ● . . .

Joanna: Do you think so? Mm — of course, she

〰 . .
doesn't approve of anyone. ● . . .

Joanna: Yes. But what d'you suggest? She won't

〰 •
enjoy anything, will she. ● . . .

Joanna: No, I asked her. I think she doesn't want to

〰 •
go anywhere. ● . . .

Joanna: I know. It's odd isn't it. Never mind. We don't

〰 •
have to go out with anyone. ● . . .

〰 . .
Joanna: In fact, let's not go out with anyone. ● . . .

Joanna: OK. Just you and me. Bye!

4·6
Do they approve of the bus service (NATURAL SPEECH) (*page 42*)

SITUATION

Bob Giddens and Brenda Smith (the first two interviewees) both have London accents.

QUESTIONS

A: this is to practise general understanding. It does not matter, at this stage, if individual words and phrases are not fully understood.

TAPESCRIPT OF EXERCISE

Interviewer: First of all I asked Bob Giddens 'What do you think of the bus service?'
Bob Giddens: My personal view on that is I come to work in my car because the bus service is so lousy. If they improved the bus service where[1] I could get home erm in the times I think reasonable I would use then use[2] the bus service, but until then, no way.[3] . . . But um yes I definitely think it can be improved by adding other routes to the town because they all spread into the town centre using the t-town centre as the . . . centre point,

• •

which[4] I think they could do more by having some ring-buses going round the outskirts of the town, because um . . . if you want to get from one side of town to the other you've got to go to the town centre, change your bus and then go on[5] to another bus to wherever you want to go; so if they had some ring-buses you could get on and go right round the outskirts of the town.

Interviewer: Mrs Smith lives in the same town and she said:
Brenda Smith: I mean I think the bus service is appalling. Luckily for me I don't use it that often[6] unless I have to go shopping.
Interviewer: What . . . how could the bus service be improved?
Brenda Smith: Well they . . . they could turn up . . . for one thing. I mean you look at a timetable and you think oh well five minutes to wait and it turns out to be an hour. which is not very nice when you are in a hurry.

Interviewer: Then I asked Pam Campbell, 'How often do you use the bus service?'
Pam Campbell: Well. fortunately. I don't have to use the bus service too often because a girl who works in my office gives me a lift into work, but I must admit when I do . . . use it I-I curse it very often. I have waited at times up to fifty minutes at the station for a bus that goes in my direction and then I have to t-walk some fifteen minutes at the end of

• •

it and I think there should be some way of warning people when a bus is *not* going to arrive and certainly much more frequent bus services.

NOTES

1 where = so that (non-standard)
2 use then use = then use (slip of the tongue)
3 no way = not at all, certainly not (informal)
4 which = but, whereas (slip of the tongue)
5 go on = get on (slip of the tongue)
6 that often = so often (informal)

NOTE ALSO

Typical features of Bob's London accent

	standard English		London accent
1	that	pronounced	tha'
2	my		mi
3	way		wy
4	but um		bu'um
	it can		i'can
5	having		'avin'
6	had		'ad

Typical features of Brenda's London accent

	standard English		London accent
1	appalling	pronounced	appallin'
2	that often		tha'often
3	have		'ave
4	well		weu

KEY

A None of them approves of the bus service. None of them *usually* travels to work by bus, though Brenda goes by bus when she goes shopping.

B1*a*) lousy 1*b*) very bad 2*a*) as it is now

2*b*) as Bob thinks it should be

3 opinion 4 people in general
C1*a*) appalling 1*b*) very bad 2*a*) the buses 2*b*) arrive 3 to wait
D1 in someone else's car 2 opinion

5·1
Who is going to do it?
(*page* 45)

PRACTICE POINT

It is very important to hear and understand the difference between these two structures, because what we say and do will depend on which structure we have heard.

E.g.	A	**I'd** telephone her as soon as possible. (= advice)
	B	Yes, alright, I will. (**B** should then telephone her)
	A	**I'll** telephone her as soon as possible. (= statement of future intention)
	B	Yes, alright. (**A** will then telephone her)

TAPESCRIPT OF EXERCISE

Examples. First, just listen to Mike and Christine talking. When is Mike advising Christine to do something? When is he offering to do something himself?

Christine: What on earth am I going to do with all these, Mike?
Mike: Oh, I'll move them. ●
Response: Oh, will you! Good.
Guide voice: Oh, will you! Good.
Christine: And what about the letter?
Mike: I think I'd throw it away. ●
Response: OK, I will.
Guide voice: OK, I will.

Now do the exercise. After each BLEEP, say 'OK, I will' or 'Oh, will you! Good.'

Christine: And I'm a bit worried about this enormous bill.
Mike: Yes, it's a problem, isn't it. However, I think I'd pay it first and then argue. ●
Response: _____
Guide voice: OK, I will.
Christine: Oh, look, Mike. What shall we do next with this new Swiss customer?
Mike: Yes, well. I'd get his order posted as soon as possible. ●
Response: _____
Guide voice: OK, I will.
Christine: But what about the Paris office? They said *they* wanted to deal with it.
Mike: Yeah, that's right. Yes, well, under the circumstances, I think I'll phone them first thing tomorrow. ●
Response: _____
Guide voice: Oh, will you! Good.
Christine: Now, we ought to do something about a new Office Manager, you know, Mike.

Mike: Yes, I know. I'll try to draft the advertisement this afternoon. ●
Response: _____
Guide voice: Oh, will you! Good.
Christine: The other thing I've been wondering about is the holiday arrangements for this year.
Mike: Well, I think I'd put a list up as soon as possible. ●
Response: _____
Guide voice: OK, I will.

What is she talking about?
(*page* 46)

PRACTICE POINT

Understanding the *general* topic of a conversation is an important skill.

DOING THE EXERCISE

Item 4 'the actor' = 'the most popular actor' or 'the best one'. ('The' stressed in this way is very frequent in spoken English. E.g. *the* film, *the* place to go to)

TAPESCRIPT OF EXERCISE

Listen to Maggie talking to Joanna. What is Maggie advising her about? After each BLEEP, write or draw your answer in the Workbook.

Maggie: Yeees . . . well, of course, I know. I thought *every*body knew. How d'you like them? That's the first thing to decide. If you like the white part hard and the yellow part soft, the best way to do it is to put it in a pan of cold water and then when the water's boiling, you cook it for . . . well for about 2½ minutes . . . oh and if the shell cracks, add a bit of salt . . . (*fade*) ● . . .

Maggie: Yes, you poor thing, you must be feeling awful . . . Last time I went to mine he told me that most kinds you buy in the shops are absolutely useless anyway. *He* said that the best way, apparently, is to put some salt on your brush and then you just brush them in the usual way. When you've finished, you're supposed to rinse your mouth out with cold water. Well, I can tell you . . . Mmm? . . . ● . . .

Maggie: Are you really? You lucky girl . . . but you ought to be careful, you know . . . with your fair skin, you may go red very quickly . . . and it's *very* painful. The best way is not to stay out for more than about half an hour when you first arrive . . . and make sure you *cover* yourself with sun oil or something. ● . . .

Maggie: Yes, it is, it's wonderful, but if you want to get in, the best thing to do is go and wait in the queue . . . Yes, I know, . . . there's nothing worse, but everybody's going . . . he's *the* actor at the moment and if you want to get a seat, it's the only way. ● . . .

KEY

Example
Spectacles.

Exercises
1 Boiling eggs.
2 Toothpaste, cleaning teeth.
3 Sunbathing.
4 A film or play.

FOR THE TEACHER: FURTHER PRACTICE

Let your students listen to a recording of someone telling a story in English. (The story should be exciting, interesting or funny!) Encourage them not to worry about the meaning of individual unknown words. At the end of the recording get them to summarise the story either orally or in writing (in general terms).

5·3
What is she trying to say?
(*page* 47)

PRACTICE POINT

Indirectness is a typically British way of being polite.

TAPESCRIPT OF EXERCISE

Examples. First, just listen to Joanna.
Is she going to make a request, or is she
going to give her advice?

Joanna: Oh, hello . . . it's Joanna here. Look, will you
be passing the – er – Post Office on your way back
to lunch . . . ? ● . . .

Joanna: Yes . . . I see . . . well, look, if you don't mind
my saying so . . . ● . . .

Now do the exercise. After each BLEEP, tick the
appropriate box in the Workbook.

Joanna: Oh, I see. You'll be going to Birmingham?
Oh! D'you think you'll be driving? ● . . .

Joanna: But on your way, I um I don't suppose you
could do me a favour, could you . . . ● . . .

Joanna: Goodness – er, well, you can tell me to mind
my own business, of course, but . . . ● . . .

Joanna: Yes, well, I *know* it's nothing to do with me
but – er . . . ● . . .

Joanna: Right. . . . OK, I'll see you at lunch . . . one
o'clock alright? . . . good . . . oh, just a minute . . .
I don't suppose you're going near the supermarket
are you? ● . . .

Joanna: Oh, you aren't . . . Oh, really? . . . well,
I think if I were you . . . ● . . .

KEY

EXAMPLES

EXERCISE

Is she asking why?
Or is she making a
suggestion? (page 49)

PRACTICE POINT

1 'Why won't you' = 'why do you refuse to'.

2 Recognising and understanding the difference
between these two structures is important, because
each needs a different response from us.

> E.g. *A* Why won't you let him drive the car?
> *B* Because he's a terrible driver, that's why.
>
> *A* Why don't you let him drive the car?
> *B* Mm, that's a good idea.
> *or*
> *B* No, I don't want to do that really.

TAPESCRIPT OF EXERCISE

Examples. First, just listen to Joanna. When is she
asking for a reason? When is she making a suggestion?

Joanna: Why won't you come with us tomorrow?
● . . .
Joanna: Well, why don't you ask him for a day off?
● . . .

Now do the exercise. After each BLEEP, tick the
appropriate box in the Workbook.

Joanna: Why won't you speak to him? ● . . .
Joanna: No, I can't see that at all, Peter. Why don't
you take a day off without telling him? ● . . .
Joanna: No, you know you don't have to. Why don't
you just come for the weekend? ● . . .
Joanna: Yes, you said that last time, if I remember
right. Why won't you come and meet them?
I think you're being very unkind. ● . . .
Joanna: Well, if you feel that way, why don't you tell
her about it? ● . . .
Joanna: Why won't you try? ● . . .
Joanna: Well, anyway, I can't go on now. I've got to
pack. See you next week. Bye.

KEY

EXAMPLES

1 *Joanna:* Why won't you come with us tomorrow? ● . . .

	1	2
Why?	✓	
I suggest . . .		

2 *Joanna:* Well, why don't you ask him for a day off? ● . . .

	1	2
Why?		
I suggest . . .		✓

EXERCISE

	1	2	3	4	5	6
Why?	✓			✓		✓
I suggest . . .		✓	✓		✓	

5·5
Which is she to do? (*page* 51)

PRACTICE POINT

1 'Or rather' is used frequently in informal spoken English, to indicate a change of mind.

TAPESCRIPT OF EXERCISE

Examples. First, just listen to Maggie. What does she want Pat to do?

Pat: There's another letter from Mr Smith, today, Miss Parkin.

Maggie: Oh Lord, yes. Look, could you send him a Spanish brochure, or rather send him ten of the things. ● . . .

Pat: Yes, right. I'll do that.

Maggie: And send them *first* class rather than second. ● . . .

Now do the exercises. After each BLEEP, complete Pat's notes on what she has to do, in the Workbook.

Pat: I was wondering, Miss Parkin, what you wanted me to do about your hotel tour.

Maggie: Yes, that's got to be sorted out, hasn't it. I think you'd better arrange something with the Italian hotels rather than the Spanish ones this year. ● . . .

Pat: Who shall I write to, to let them know you're coming?

Maggie: Oh . . . write to the Managers, would you, or rather phone them. ● . . .

Pat: Right . . . what shall I do if I can't speak to the Manager?

Maggie: Well then, ask to speak to somebody else . . . the receptionist rather than the local representative . . . and leave a message. ● . . .

Pat: How long shall I book you in for?

Maggie: Oh, I'd say about a night at each, or rather two. ● . . .

Pat: Very well, Miss Parkin. And if you'll tell me how you'll be travelling, I'll get your tickets and things.

Maggie: Oh, that would be very good. Could you organise something by plane . . . or rather by plane and then car. ● . . .

Pat: Yes, of course. Is that all for now? . . .

Maggie: Yes, thank you, Pat. Oh, just one last thing, could you get me some black coffee rather than white.

KEY

Examples
1 Ten Spanish brochures.
2 First class.

Exercises
1 The Italian hotels.
2 Phone.
3 Receptionist.
4 Two nights at each hotel.
5 Plane and then car.

5·6
Who's going to do what?
(NATURAL SPEECH) (*page* 53)

TAPESCRIPT OF EXERCISE

A *Jan:* Carol.
Carol: Yes.
Jan: Um, Jan.
Carol: Yes, Jan.
Jan: I wonder if you could do something for me, erm, this retained adviser's contract. . . .
Carol: Yeah.

• •

Jan: needs drawing up erm . . . I think that probably the best thing . . .
Jan: Why don't you ask Meg what the formula is . . .
Jan: So erm if I was you[1] I'd, yes, ask Meg . . .
Carol: Aha.

• •

Jan: and then I think it's just a question of asking David Lee to fix it up. I'll do a note to erm Mrs . . . Laird to tell her that that's what we're doing.
Carol: Yeah.
Jan: Erm and if you could ask David to let us have it back as soon as he can, erm I'd be very grateful. . . .

B *Wendy:* Wendy Searle.
Annie: Hello, (*Wendy:* Yes.) Annie here.
Wendy: Oh, hello, Annie.
Annie: I wonder if you could do a couple of things for me.
Wendy: Yes
Annie: Erm first of all, you know[2] those um those brochures. . . .
Wendy: Yes
Annie: Well, I wonder if you could do me ten copies of them, please, um quite urgently. Um I'd go down to the machine downstairs, because I went upstairs a moment ago and it was really crowded . . . masses of people.
Wendy: Fine. OK.
Annie: OK and the other thing is um if you're going to the stationery office . . .

C *Elisabeth:* Hello?
Chris: Hello, Elisabeth?
Elisabeth: Yeh.
Chris: It's Chris here.
Elisabeth: Oh, hello, Chris.
Chris: Could you please make out a Company cheque to Jane Haggerty.
Elisabeth: Mhm. Is that . . . hang on . . . that double 'g'.
Chris: That's it, yes.

Elisabeth: Ya.
Chris: E-R-T-Y.
Elisabeth: Mm.
Chris: . . . for £22·75 pence.
Elisabeth: Mhm.
Chris: It's for some secretarial work.
Elisabeth: Mmm.
Chris: She's actually sent in two invoices but we could have just one cheque rather than two.

NOTES

if I was you = if I were you (informal)
you know = a phrase often used to introduce a subject (informal)

NOTE ALSO

1 Asking people to do things:

I wonder if you could . . . . . . (polite)
If you could . . . . . . I'd be grateful (polite/formal)
Could you please . . . . . . (polite/formal)

2 Identifying on the telephone:
E.g. *Person answering:* Wendy Searle.
Caller: Hello; Annie here.

E.g. *Person answering:* Hello?
Caller: Hello; it's Chris here.

KEY

A 1*a)* opinion 1*b)* give Carol some advice
2*a)* don't 2*b)* a suggestion 3*a)* I'd
3*b)* She wants Carol to ask Meg. 4 opinion
5*a)* I'll 5*b)* She will do a note herself.

B 1 the brochures 2*a)* I'd 2*b)* She wants Wendy to go to the machine. 3*a)* masses 3*b)* There are lots of people wanting to use the machine. 4 She's going to ask Wendy to do something.

C 1*a)* make out 1*b)* write 2 Haggerty/£22.75
3 one